THE ILLUSTRATED DICTIONARY OF

SAILING

THE ILLUSTRATED DICTIONARY OF
SAILING

Jane Daniels

GALLERY BOOKS
An Imprint of W.H. Smith Publishers Inc.
112 Madison Avenue
New York, New York 10016

A FRIEDMAN GROUP BOOK

Published by GALLERY BOOKS
An imprint of W.H. Smith Publishers, Inc.
112 Madison Avenue
New York, New York 10016

ISBN 0-8317-4865-6

THE ILLUSTRATED DICTIONARY OF SAILING
was prepared and produced by
Michael Friedman Publishing Group, Inc.
15 West 26th Street
New York, New York 10010

Editor: Sharyn Rosart
Art Director: Robert W. Kosturko
Designer: Devorah Levinrad
Photography Editor: Christopher Bain
Production Manager: Karen L. Greenberg
Technical Consultants: Andrew Lance and the staff of Defender Industries, Inc.

Gallery Books are available for bulk purchase for sales promotions and premium use. For
details write or telephone the Manager of Special Sales, W.H. Smith Publishers, Inc.,
112 Madison Avenue, New York, New York 10016. (212) 532-6600

Typeset by Mar + X Myles
Color separations by Universal Colour Scanning Ltd.
Printed and bound in Hong Kong by Leefung-Asco Printers Ltd.

Acknowledgments

This book has greatly benefited from the generous
assistance of others, and it is a pleasure to
acknowledge them here.

The project would have been extremely difficult without
the patient and unending help of Andrew Lance. He
answered numerous questions, provided constant
guidance, and willingly reviewed every
aspect of the book.

For assistance in the research of key details, I would like
to thank the United States Coast Guard, the United States
Yacht Racing Union, *Woodenboat* magazine, *Sailing
World* magazine, Robert Weir, and Hal Tweedy, general
manager of Defender Industries, Incorporated,
and his staff.

For their support and encouragement along the way,
thanks go to Margaret Allen, Jeb Beaudin, Katherine
Khan, Tom O'Hara, Marc Perman, and Susan Tufankjian.
I also extend deep appreciation to my father, William B.
Daniels, and Ann Marshall, who gave me a comfortable
corner to write in when I needed it the most.
Finally, I would like to thank the book's editor, Sharyn
Rosart, and, for her care over the design,
Devorah Levinrad.

This book

is dedicated to

Jim O'Hara (1925–1989)

CONTENTS

THE ILLUSTRATED DICTIONARY OF
SAILING

Introduction

Introduction *This book will help you understand the "language of the sea." Unless you learn the words and expressions used on boats and in talking and reading about them, you won't be able to fully enjoy the pleasures of getting out on the water and going sailing.*

The simple appeal of relying only on the natural elements of wind and water to generate movement is what attracts many people to sailing. Others may be interested in sailing as an intensely competitive sport that presents both strenuous physical demands and the intellectual challenges of strategy and tactics. For the casual day-sailor or the vigorous participant, knowledge of the appropriate vocabulary is essential.

Nothing gives me greater pride as a sailing instructor than to work with a novice who begins timidly and grows in confidence and

ability as he or she starts to appreciate the finer points of the sport.

As a commentator for many different types of sailboat racing events, I've noticed how the reactions of spectators unfamiliar with sailing change once I begin calling their attention to starting line strategy, the precision of a tacking duel, the spinnaker action around a jibe mark, and offensive and defensive tactical maneuvers.

Whether enjoying a leisurely cruise or watching or participating in a regatta, the assimilation of nautical terminology will increase your knowledge and understanding of basic boat handling and sailing techniques.

Happy sailing.

Lou Carretero

Instructor, Steve Colgate's Offshore Sailing School

The Dictionary

Abaft
Behind or toward the *stern* of a boat.

Abeam
At right angles to the *centerline* of a boat.

Adrift
Free-floating, without mooring or means of propulsion.

Aft
At, near, or toward the *stern*.

Afterpart
The part of a boat *aft* of the *beam*.

Aground
On the shore or bottom of a body of water; a boat stranded this way is said to have run *aground*.

Ahull
When a boat is *hove-to* with all its sails lowered, or *furled*.

This boat has run aground and will have to wait for the next rise in tide before floating off.

© Roger Garwood/Wheeler Pictures

During the past forty years the America's Cup has been raced in 12-meters like the one shown here.

Alee

Toward the side of a boat that is opposite the source of the wind.

All standing

To have all sails flying when *running* before the wind.

Aloft

Overhead.

America's Cup

One of the most celebrated of sporting trophies, this elaborate baroque cup was made by Robert Garrard, Jr., of London in 1848. It was originally called the Hundred Guinea Cup. This name may derive from its original cost (about $525 U.S. at the exchange rate at that time) or from the purse that accompanied it. In 1851, the Royal Yacht Squadron issued a general challenge to an American yacht to compete in a regatta held in connection with the Crystal Palace Exhibition in London. The New York Yacht Club built a 101-foot (30-meter) schooner, *America*, which was launched on May 3, 1851. *America* finished so far ahead of the English yachts that the trophy was henceforth known as the America's Cup.

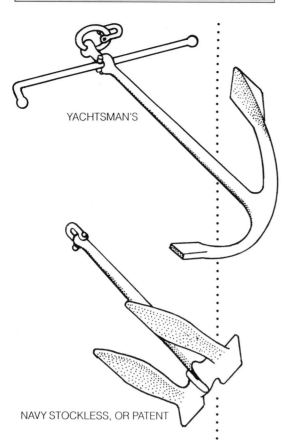

YACHTSMAN'S

NAVY STOCKLESS, OR PATENT

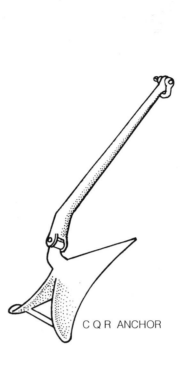

C Q R ANCHOR

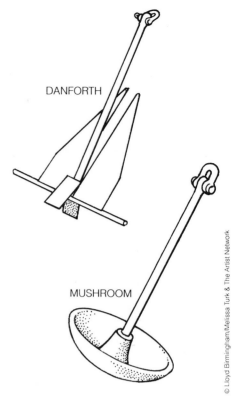

DANFORTH

MUSHROOM

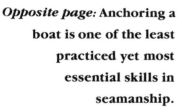

Opposite page: **Anchoring a boat is one of the least practiced yet most essential skills in seamanship.**

Anchor

A piece of metal equipment, used for securing a boat to the seabed. Among the common types of anchors are the Danforth, plow, mushroom, yachtsman's, and grapnel. See also *holding ground*; compare *sea anchor*.

Anchorage

A suitable place for anchoring. An anchorage should be sheltered from the wind, strong tide, and currents.

Anchor's aweigh

Command signaling the act of raising *anchor*.

Anchor light

A white light, usually on the *forestay*, required at night *anchorages*.

Anemometer

Instrument to measure wind speed.

Anticyclone

A high-pressure area where cold, dense air sinks and becomes warmer. The air currents in an anticyclone flow clockwise in the northern hemisphere and counterclockwise in the southern hemisphere.

Antifoulant

Paint additive that contains copper or chemical agents to impede the growth of algae, weeds, and *barnacles* when applied to a boat's bottom.

© Onne Van Der Wal

This boat is moving under auxiliary power.

Opposite page: Barometers.

Aport_____
To the left, or *port*, side of a boat.

Apparent wind_____
The speed and direction of the wind felt aboard a moving boat; the combination of the *true wind* and boat speed.

Ashore_____
On or to the shore.

Aspect ratio_____
Relationship between the height of a sail and its length. A tall, narrow sail is said to have a high *aspect ratio*, while a less tall and wider sail is said to have a low *aspect ratio*.

Astern_____
Toward a vessel's *stern*.

Athwartship_____
At right angles to a boat's *centerline*.

Autopilot_____
An electronic, hydraulic, or mechanical steering device generally incorporating a *compass*. When attached to a boat's steering mechanism, it maintains the boat on a constant *course*.

Auxiliary_____
A permanently installed engine used to power a sailboat.

B

Back a sail

To hold a sail so that the wind fills it from the opposite side; used to slow down a boat or to force a boat onto a *tack* if it is *in irons*.

Backing wind

A counterclockwise change in the wind direction; for example, from north to northwest. Compare *veering*.

Backstay

A rigging wire, fitted to control or prevent forward movement of the *mast*, which can be used to vary the amount of bend in the mast.

Backwinded

To have the wind on one *tack* filling the sails, which are *trimmed* for the other tack. See *by the lee*.

Bail

To remove water from a boat.

Ballast

Heavy material, usually lead or iron, that is placed in the *bilge* or on the *keel* to provide stability. Often the only ballast on smaller sailboats is the crew.

Barber hauler

An adjustment for a *jib sheet*, sliding along the jib sheet between the *clew* of the *jib* and *fairlead*, used to change the sheeting angle.

Bare poles

To sail with no sails set, usually in a very strong wind, strong enough to move the boat by the force on the *mast* and the *boom* (the "poles") alone.

Barnacles

Small, hard-shelled marine animals that cling to pilings, docks, and the bottoms of boats.

Barney post

Short post in the *cockpit* fitted with a *block* and *cam cleat* for the main *sheet*.

Barometer

Instrument for measuring atmospheric pressure.

Courtesy Gardener & Co./Wempe Products (all photos)

Barratry

A term in maritime law referring to a fraudulent breach of duty by a ship's captain, to the injury of the ship's owner or cargo, for example, the scuttling of a vessel or theft of cargo.

Battens

Thin, flexible strips fitted into pockets in a sail to maintain its shape, or *camber*. Battens can be made of wood, plastic, fiberglass, or metal.

Beach

To drive a vessel onto the shore.

Beacon

A navigational marker, usually on land.

Beam

The width of a boat at its widest point.

Beam reach

See *points of sail*.

Bear away; bear off

To change course away from the wind. Also described as *falling off*.

Bearing

The direction to an object from a boat measured relative to the boat's *course* or to *compass* degrees.

Bear off

To turn away from the wind, or to *leeward*.

Beat

To sail to *windward*, *close-hauled*, *tacking* as you go.

Beaufort wind scale

A universally recognized system of classifying wind *velocity*, developed by Sir Francis Beaufort (1774–1857) of the Royal Navy, ranging from flat calm (0) to survival conditions (10 and upwards). See Appendix.

Becalmed

To be left motionless by lack of wind.

Belay

To make fast a line around a *cleat* or *belaying pin*, usually with a *figure-eight knot*.

Belaying pin

A sturdy wooden or metal pin fitted onto the side of a boat or by the mast, used to secure *halyards* and other lines.

Bend

Tying two lines together with a knot; to bend a sail means to fasten a sail to the *boom* and *mast*.

Bermuda rig

Same as *Marconi rig*. See *Sailboat rig*.

Opposite page: Most sails have a set of battens, which help achieve a correct sail shape by supporting the sail's roach.

Sailing towards an objective directly upwind requires beating, a series of tacks on an upwind course.

WIND

© Lloyd Birmingham/Melissa Turk & The Artist Network

A line belayed around a cleat.

© Daniella Jo Nilva

Bernoulli's principle

If the speed, or velocity, of the air or fluid flowing past one side of an airfoil (such as a *sail* or *keel*) is greater than that on the other side, the pressure correspondingly decreases on the first side, thus creating a force flowing from the higher pressure area to the lower pressure area. This principle applies not only to wind moving across a sail but also to water flowing around a keel.

Berth

An assigned docking or mooring position. Also, a place where a person sleeps on board.

Bight

A loop or bend in a *line*. Also, a bend in the shoreline.

Bilge

The area inside a boat beneath the *cockpit* or *cabin* floor. The water that may collect there is known as bilge water.

The compass is mounted in a binnacle, the domed case on top of the wheel pedestal.

Binnacle

A case, usually mounted on a pedestal, containing a *compass* that can be seen by the *helmsman*.

Bitt

A short post attached to a *dock* or a boat's *deck* used to secure mooring lines.

Bitter end

Last inboard link of an anchor chain or anchor line. Also, the extreme end of a line. If a line is paid out to the bitter end, there is nothing beyond it.

Blanket

The effect of a boat positioned directly *upwind* of a *downwind* boat, thus "stealing the wind" from the downwind boat.

Block

Nautical term for a pulley. A block may include more than one *sheave* to increase its mechanical advantage.

A double block.

© Allan Weitz

© Allan Weitz

Top: The boom supports the foot of the mainsail while allowing the sail to travel freely across the boat while tacking or jibing.

Courtesy Hall Spars/photo by George Glod

Above: A boom vang.

Blooper

An L-shaped sail that may be flown simultaneously with a spinnaker on a *broad reach* or a *run* on the *leeward* side of the boat to increase the area of the sails in use.

Board

To climb or walk onto a boat.

Boat hook

A pole for catching hold of another boat or a *mooring*.

Bolt rope

A reinforcing rope along the *luff* or *foot* of a sail.

Boom

A *spar* to which the *foot* of a sail is attached.

Boom vang

A *tackle* or hydraulic device secured to the *boom* to prevent it from rising.

Bosun's chair

A canvas or wooden seat used by sailors while at work *aloft*.

Bow

Forward end of a boat.

Bowditch

Common reference to the *American Practical Navigator,* originally written by Nathaniel Bowditch (1773–1838). This compendium of navigational information is encyclopedic and should be included in any serious sailing library.

Bowline

A mooring *line* attached to the bow. Also called a *painter* on small sailboats and dinghys.

Bowsprit

A *spar* extending from the *bow* of some boats, allowing a *headsail* to be secured farther forward, thus providing additional sail area.

Breakers

Waves broken by *shoals*, reefs, or ledges, or those that smash against a rocky shore.

Breakwater

An artificial barrier to protect an *anchorage* or harbor.

Break ground

To break an *anchor* loose from the bottom.

Breast lines

Mooring lines, usually fore and aft, which are led at right angles to the side of a boat.

Brightwork

All varnished woodwork and polished metal fittings.

Below: **The strong steel frame at the bow is called the pulpit, which is bolted onto the foredeck. Crew can brace themselves against it while changing headsails.**

Left: **This crew member is being hoisted aloft in a bosun's chair.**

BELL

CAN

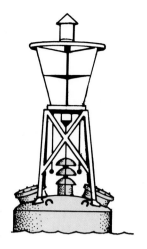

LIGHT AND SOUND

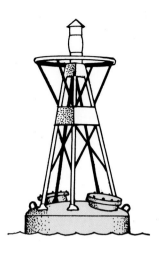

LIGHT

Broach

The result of losing control of a boat's *helm* while sailing *downwind*. A gust can cause a boat to *heel* at such an angle that there is insufficient helm to hold the boat on course, thus forcing the boat to round up sharply to *weather*.

Broad reach

See *points of sail*.

Bulkhead

Any vertical *partition* on a boat.

Bulwarks

The sides of a boat above deck level.

Buoy

A floating marker that indicates channels, banks, or potential underwater hazards. Buoys are maintained by the Coast Guard. The permanent location of each buoy is shown on a *chart*, which also includes a description of the buoy (its shape, color, signaling device, and number). The various types of buoys are described below.

Bell buoys are markers that contain one or more bells that ring as waves rock them. In newer models, the bells are struck by compressed gas or an electrically operated hammer.

Can buoys are cylindrical markers that are usually odd-numbered and painted black or green.

NUN

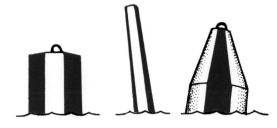

SPECIAL PURPOSE BUOYS

Combination buoys are markers in which a light and sound signal are combined, such as a lighted *bell buoy* or a lighted *horn buoy.*

Flashing buoys are markers that show one or more flashes of light at regular intervals.

Nun buoys are cylindrical markers with conical tops that are usually even-numbered and painted red.

Sound buoys are markers that provide a sound signal useful in periods of poor visibility, whether caused by darkness or fog. The sound mechanism may be operated by the motion of the sea or by a battery.

Special-purpose buoys are those that mark anchorage areas, dredging or diving operations, fishnet areas, and the like.

Buoyancy
Flotation capability.

Burgee
A small signal pennant identifying the yacht club to which a boat owner belongs.

By the lee
To be *running* before the wind with the breeze coming over the same side of the boat that the *boom* is on. Sailing by the lee is often caused by the *helmsman* steering too far *downwind,* and an accidental *jibe* is frequently a consequence.

A basic cruiser's cabin may contain a galley (as shown here), chart table, stowage space, head, and berths located in the forepeak and the cabin proper.

© Allan Weitz

Cabin

Livable space beneath the *deck* of a boat.

Calm

Wind speed under one knot.

Camber

The curvature of a sail.

Capsize

To turn over in the water. Capsizing is not uncommon in any unballasted boat. All *dinghies* generally have some form of *buoyancy* to prevent them from sinking, and the placement of this buoyancy plays a critical role in determining the ease with which a capsized boat can be righted. A boat normally capsizes to *leeward*: it heels over to the point where water pours in over the *gunwale*, and capsizes. A boat will often float level in the water when capsized, with the sails and *mast* lying on the water and the *centerboard* sticking about a foot out of the water. The *helmsman* and crew should never leave a capsized boat; it will often float away faster than a person can swim.

* * *

There are many ways to right a capsized boat, but the one described below is easy to learn and well-proven.

* * *

The centerboard should be fully down, and the *rudder* checked to make sure that it is still attached to its fitting. The helmsman should swim around the boat to the centerboard, using the *mainsheet* as a safety line. The crew then swims to the inside of the boat, locates the end of the *jib sheet*, and throws it to the helmsman. The crew then holds onto the boat while the helmsman pulls himself up onto the centerboard, using the jib sheet for balancing. Standing on the centerboard and leaning back, he pulls the jib sheet to start the righting movement. As the boat comes out of the water, the helmsman will be able to reach the gunwale and clamber over the side of the boat. The crew, already scooped aboard, can help him if necessary.

* * *

This scoop method will also work if a boat capsizes to *windward*. If this is the case, the boat's rig will be pointing into the wind, thus causing the sails to fill with air as the boat is being righted, possibly causing it to capsize again—to leeward—

Left: Note that the sailors from this capsized boat are staying with the boat.

as a result. The heaviest person should be scooped into the boat, and the person on the centerboard should drop into the water as soon as the boat begins to right itself. The person in the boat should move his or her weight to windward to help prevent a leeward capsize.

* * *

Some dinghies turn bottom side up, or *turn turtle*, quite easily. To right a boat in this position the helmsman and crew must first turn it onto its side (with its rig pointing to leeward) by kneeling on the side of the boat and pulling on the centerboard and jib sheet. After the boat comes into a horizontal position it can be righted by the method described above.

Cast off
To let go any lines securing a sailboat to a fixed mooring, dock, or another boat.

Catamaran
A twin-hulled boat.

Catboat, cat rig
A single-masted sailboat that carries only a *mainsail*. The mast is positioned near the *bow*.

Cat's paws
Ruffled patches of water produced by light breezes on a calm day.

Caulk
Substance used to make seals watertight.

Above: Some different types of catamarans include the Hobie, Tornado, Stiletto, Nacra, Prindle, and Dart.

CENTERBOARD

Centerboard

A plate that is pinned at the forward end and pivots through the bottom of a boat to extend into the water beneath a boat in place of a keel. See also *daggerboard*. The housing for the centerboard is called the centerboard trunk. A centerboard is a lightweight alternative to a *keel*, improving stability by slowing the rolling motion of a boat.

Centerline

The center of a boat, from *bow* to *stern*.

Chain plates

Metal fittings secured to the sides of a boat to which the *shrouds* are attached.

Channel

The navigable portion of a body of water, sometimes dredged and often marked with *buoys* to guide boats.

Charts

Nautical maps issued by governmental sources and updated periodically.

Chine

The edge formed by the intersection of the sides of a boat with its bottom. A hard chine is sharply angled; a soft chine is rounded.

Chock

A fitting attached to the *deck* through which the anchor line, *bowline*, and mooring lines may pass.

Chop

Continuous small, uneven waves.

Chronometer

A highly accurate clock or watch that can be used for navigation; comparing local time to Greenwich Mean Time will yield a ship's *longitude*.

Chute
Casual term for *spinnaker*.

Cleat
A wooden, metal, or nylon fitting for securing a line.

Clew
The lower *aft* corner, or *sheeting* end, of a fore-and-aft sail.

Clinometer
Instrument to measure a boat's *heel*, or sideways roll.

Close-hauled
See *points of sail*.

Close reach
See *points of sail*.

Above: **A standard chock.**

Left: **The sheets of the head-sail are attached to the clew, allowing the sail to be trimmed.**

Clouds

Convective, or *cumulus,* clouds are caused by rising portions of buoyant air. The air is heated by the sun, warming the land beneath it. As it rises, it expands, cools, and condenses as water droplets. Cumulus clouds are soft and cottony in appearance, and produce strong updrafts, or *thermals*. The wind is usually variable underneath this type of cloud.

*   *   *

Layer, or *stratus*, clouds are caused by the widespread lifting of stable air, and indicate the onset of a warm front, which often brings low, dark rain clouds, or *nimbostratus*. Thunderstorm, or *cumulonimbus*, clouds indicate extreme atmospheric insta-

bility and are common along cold fronts. Very strong winds from the direction of the storm and a drop in temperature are commonly seen.

*   *   *

A squall line is a series of storm clouds, generally preceded by the "calm before the storm," which is caused by damp surface air rising into the clouds. The worst gusts of a squall come with its first blast.

*   *   *

Fog is a cloud that rests on land or water. *Evaporation fog*, commonly called sea smoke, is never more than a few feet thick. *Advection fog* can be thick and widespread and can last for days. It forms when warm moist air flows over a cold surface, such as a cold ocean current.

Skies often clear at sunset, when convection clouds formed during the day disappear, or when a front passes through.

Opposite page: **Clouds, as well as the colors in the sky, are visual indications of the weather.**

Compass.

Opposite page above: As many controls as possible should be led back to the cockpit for easy access.

Clove hitch

See *knots.*

Coaming

A raised edge around a *cockpit,* designed to keep out water.

Cockpit

The area of the deck in which the *tiller* or steering wheel is located. It generally contains a seating area as well.

Come about

To bring a boat from one *tack* to the other tack when sailing into the wind. Commonly referred to as tacking, although tacking refers both to coming about and *jibing.*

Companionway

An area below deck which contains the staircase or ladder that leads to the *cabin.*

Compass

An instrument used to indicate direction in relation to the earth's magnetic field.

Compass rose

A graduated circle printed on a *chart* that has the points of the *compass.*

Compensate

To correct a compass to allow for local magnetic attraction so that it will indicate magnetic north as accurately as possible.

Cordage

General term for all kinds of line over an inch in diameter.

Corinthian

A term describing an amateur sailor or amateur event; used primarily to describe a member of a racing crew.

CLOSE-HAULED ON PORT TACK

COMING ABOUT

CLOSE-HAULED ON STARBOARD TACK

© Daniella Jo Nilva

Discovering new harbors and shorelines is one of the most enjoyable aspects of cruising.

Course_____
A boat's *heading*, or direction of travel through the water.

Crabbing_____
Making *leeway*, or moving sideways through water.

Cradle_____
A frame on which a boat rests when *ashore*.

Craft_____
General term for small boats.

Cringle_____
A ring sewn into a sail through which a *line* may be passed.

Cruiser_____
A boat with accommodations for living on board.

Crutch_____
Support for the *boom* when sails are not flying.

Cumulonimbus_____
See *clouds*.

Cumulus_____
See *clouds*.

Cunningham_____
An adjustment through an *eye* in the *luff* of a *mainsail* above the *tack*; it allows adjustment of the tension of the luff in order to move the *draft* forward or *aft*.

Current

The nontidal flow of a body of water.

Cutter

A single-masted sailboat with the mast positioned more than two-fifths of the *waterline* length *aft* of the point where the *bow* emerges from the water.

Daggerboard

A plate that can be raised or lowered vertically through the bottom of a boat. See also *centerboard*.

Daysailer

An open boat that is used for day sailing or casual racing.

Dead ahead, dead astern

Directly ahead, directly *aft*.

Dead reckoning

A system of *navigation* in which a position on a *chart* is plotted based on speed, elapsed time, and a course steered from a known position, or *fix*. This method is used in every form of navigation.

* * *

During the eighteenth and nineteenth centuries, because *charts* were scarce and expensive, ship captains did not use them to plot their *courses* and the distances they had sailed. Instead they figured a current position mathematically, using the courses and speeds sailed from a previous direction. This was called deduced reckoning, which abbreviated to ded reckoning, and eventually evolved into dead reckoning.

The daggerboard is common in very small boats as it takes up less room than a centerboard.

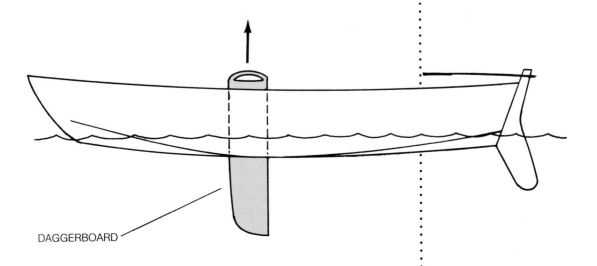

DAGGERBOARD

Deadrise

In a V-bottomed boat, the amount of the rise from where the bottom rises at an angle to a horizontal line from the keel; expressed as an angle or in inches per foot.

Deck

The covering of the interior or *cabin* of a boat.

Deep six

Nautical slang for tossing something overboard.

Departure, point of

The last known position, or *fix* noted by an outward-bound boat.

Dinghy

A small (usually under twenty feet long), undecked, single-masted racing boat; also, a rowboat or skiff, often used as a ship's *tender*.

Displacement

The weight of water displaced by a floating vessel, a measurement mainly used for ships. Sailboats are usually measured by their *waterline* length.

Displacement hull

A *hull* design that achieves its *buoyancy* by displacing a volume of water that equals the weight of the hull and its load. Compare *planing hull*.

Dock

Any platform or *pier* that boats may come alongside.

Doldrums

Parts of the ocean on either side of the equator known for their dead *calms* and light, baffling breezes.

Dory

A flat-bottomed, hard-*chined* *dinghy* with a narrow *stern* and high *freeboard*.

Downhaul

The *tackle* used for tensioning the *luff* of a sail. It should be adjusted like an *outhaul*: taut for a flat sail when sailing *upwind* or on a breezy day; and loose, for a baggier sail, when sailing *downwind* or on a calm day.

Downwind

To *leeward*.

Deck of a modern cruiser.

© Ulf Sjostedt/FPG International

© Allan Weitz

The dory is noted for its seaworthiness.

Draft

The distance from the water level to the deepest part of a boat. If a boat touches bottom in four feet of water, then its draft is four feet, or it *draws* four feet. *Centerboard* boat descriptions will usually give two drafts for a boat, one with the board up and the other with the board down. It is important to know how much water the boat draws so that the shallow areas can be avoided. Also the fullness or "belly" of a sail.

Draw

A sail is said to be drawing when it is filled with wind. Also, the minimum depth of water a boat requires; see *draft*.

Drift

To move with the *tide* or *current*.

Drifter

A *headsail* used in extremely light winds.

Drogue

A cone-shaped *sea anchor* towed by a boat in order to keep its bow pointed into the seas when *hove-to* or its stern to the seas when *running*.

© Christopher Bain

Fairleads are sometimes set into the raised edge around the deck.

Earing

A short line securing a *reefed* sail to the *boom*.

Ease

To let out a *sheet* or line slowly; opposite of *trim*.

Ebb

The outgoing, or falling, tide.

Eddy

A water or air current flowing against the main current. It often moves in a swirling, circular fashion. *Buoys* and *piers* in tidal waters can produce eddies, as do heat differences in ocean currents, for example, the Gulf Stream. Winds that form along mountainous coasts also produce eddies.

Ensign

The nautical version of a boat's national flag.

Even keel

Floating level, that is, not *listing*.

Eye

Any kind of a hole through which a *line* is led or fastened.

Fenders protecting a boat's hull.

Fairlead

A *block* that adjusts the *trim* angle of a *jib* and opening of the *slot*. Also, a hole in the *deck* through which a *line* is led.

Fair wind

Any wind that allows a sailboat to *fetch* a point without having to *tack*.

Fall off

To *bear off*, or sail a boat away from the wind.

False keel

A strip affixed to the main keel to protect it.

Fathom

A unit of measurement for depth. One fathom equals six feet (2 meters).

Fender

A cushion hung over a boat's side to prevent contact with another vessel or a dock.

Fend off

To shove off by hand or *boat hook* to avoid contact with a dock or another boat.

© Allan Weitz

Opposite page: **To flemish a line is one way to ensure that it dries properly.**

Line running through a fitting.

Fetch

To sail *close-hauled* to an objective without having to *tack*. To fetch a mark is the same as to lay a mark.

Fiberglass

Cloth made of glass filaments, used in conjunction with resin for boat construction and repair.

Figure-eight knot

See *knots*.

Fittings

Hardware.

Fix

An accurate position determined by celestial or land observation.

Flemish

To coil a line in a spiral fashion, laid flat on a deck.

Flood

A rising tide.

Flotsam

Floating wreckage or debris. See also *jetsam*.

Flukes

The points or wings of certain types of *anchors* that dig into the seabed.

Fog

See *clouds*.

Following sea

A sea that is traveling in the same direction as a boat. Compare *head sea*.

The distance from the top of a boat's hull to the waterline is called freeboard.

The foot of the mainsail is attached to the boom.

Foot _____
The lower edge of a sail.

Fore _____
Toward, near, or at the end of the *bow.* Compare *aft.*

Fore-and-aft _____
In line from *bow* to *stern.*

Foredeck _____
The part of the *deck* forward of the *mast.*

Forepeak _____
A space below *deck* in the *bow* of a boat.

Foresail *(pronounced for-s'l)* _____
Triangular sail set forward of the *mast.*

Forestay _____
A *stay* leading from the top of the *mast* to the *bow* to control or prevent backward movement of the mast.

Foul _____
To twist, entangle, or obstruct.

Founder _____
To fill with water and sink; said of a boat.

Free _____
To cast off or untangle.

Freeboard _____
The part of a boat's *hull* that is not submerged.

Furl _____
To roll a sail while it is secured to its *boom* or *spar.*

G

Gaff

A *spar* to which the top side of a four-sided sail is secured.

Gaff rig

See *sailboat rig*.

Galley

Nautical term for a kitchen.

Gangplank

A movable bridge or walkway used to walk from a dock or pier to a boat.

Gather way

The act of moving forward as wind fills the sails.

General recall

A *race committee's* decision to abandon the start of a race when there are several undefined premature starters or a mistake in starting procedure.

Genoa

A large *jib*, or headsail, whose *clew* overlaps the *mainsail*; also called a *jenny*.

Ghosting

Moving in a flat calm when there is no *apparent wind*.

Larger headsails, like the genoa seen here, are used to increase sail area for greater speed.

Gimbals

A system by which an object—a compass, barometer, or lamp, for example—is suspended so that it will remain level when its base of support is tipped.

Gooseneck

A fitting that connects the boom to the *mast*. The *gooseneck* allows the boom to move in any direction. It can either be fixed or sliding.

Goosewing

To sail downwind with the *mainsail* set on one side of the boat and the *jib* on the opposite side. Also called *wing-on-wing*.

Grommet

A rope or metal ring sewn into a sail or hammered into a tarpaulin.

Gudgeon

A socket bolted onto the *transom* or sternposts of a boat with a removable rudder, into which a *pintle* fits.

Gunkholing

A slang term for shallow-water sailing.

Gunwale *(pronounced gunnel)*

The upper edge of the side of the *hull*.

Guy

Steadying line or wire. When used for a spinnaker pole it is called the foreguy or topping lift. Also, the *spinnaker sheet* on the *windward* side of the boat.

Halyard

A line or wire used to hoist a sail. It is usually attached to a sail with a U-shaped fitting called a *shackle*. Halyards are considered part of the *running rigging*.

Hand

A crew member. The call "all hands" commands all crew members to assist an overburdened *watch*.

Hank

A plastic or stainless steel snap used to attach the *jib* to the *forestay*. Hanks permit the sail to be raised or lowered rapidly and neatly.

Hard alee

A command to *come about*.

Harden up

To sail a boat closer to the wind.

Hatch

An opening in a *deck*, fitted with a cover.

Hauser

A heavy *line* or cable used for *mooring*, docking, or towing a boat.

Head

Nautical term for a toilet. Also, the top of a sail.

Header

A shift in wind direction toward the *bow* of the boat.

Heading

The direction in which a boat is pointing.

The gunwale is where the hull and deck meet, so called because the upper guns of a fighting vessel were pointed from it.

Headsail

A sail set forward of the mast. Types of headsails include *jibs*, *genoas*, *drifters*, and *staysails*. They are distinguished by their cut, weight, and size.

Head sea

A sea that is traveling in a direction opposite the direction of a boat. Compare *following sea*.

Head-to-wind

To place a boat's *bow* into the wind.

Head up

To sail closer to the wind; also described as *hardening up* or "coming up."

Headway

Moving ahead.

The type of headsail used depends on the strength of the wind and the size of the waves.

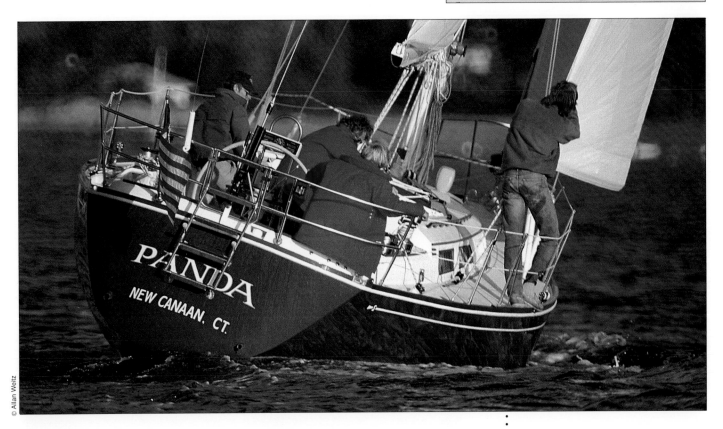

© Allan Weitz

Heave

To pull or haul together.

Heave to

To bring a boat to a standstill by *backing* the *headsail* and lashing the *tiller*.

Heaving line

Small line with a weighted bag or cluster of line on the end tossed to someone on shore when docking, to another boat, or to a man overboard.

Heel

The tilt or *list* of a vessel. A boat is said to be heeling when it leans over at an angle while sailing. The greater the angle between the boat's course and the wind, the less its tendency to heel.

Helm

The steering apparatus on a boat, either a *tiller* or a steering wheel.

Helmsman

The crew member who steers.

High

An area of high barometric pressure, generally accompanied by sunny skies and light breezes. Also, to sail high is to sail close to the wind.

High and dry

A vessel *aground* above the high-water mark.

The heeling of a boat under sail is one of the most distinctive aspects of sailing.

With the boat head-to-wind, the mainsail can be hoisted.

Hiking requires stamina and concentration to keep a boat upright in strong winds.

Hike

To sit on the side of a boat and lean out to counteract excessive *heeling*. It requires agility and concentration.

Hiking straps

Fore-and-aft straps attached to the floorboards or *centerboard* trunk used by crew members while hiking out to secure themselves by hooking their feet under the straps.

Hogging moment

Position of a vessel when a wave is under its middle.

Hoist

To raise a sail.

Hold

Storage space below *deck*, for cargo, supplies, or line.

Holding ground

The part of the seabed where the *anchor* digs in.

Holystone

A soft, porous sandstone used to scrub wooden *decks*.

Horse latitudes

Two high-pressure regions, about thirty degrees north and thirty degrees south *latitude*, characterized by calms and very light winds. Horses and other livestock being transported to other parts of the world would die during slow passages through these areas of prolonged calm.

Hove down

Excessive *heeling*. Also the process of scraping a boat's bottom.

Hull

The part of a boat from the *deck* down. The hull can be made from a wide variety of materials, including wood, plastic, *fiberglass*, or metal.

Hull speed

The theoretical maximum speed a *displacement* boat can attain from wind power. Usually the larger the boat, the faster it will go.

Inboard

Toward the center of a boat.

In irons; in stays

A boat is said to be in irons when it has stopped moving because it is pointing directly into the wind. This can happen when a boat attempts a *tack*, is stopped by a wave or loss of momentum when turning through the wind and thus loses *headway*.

In the wind

Pointed too high, or *pinching*.

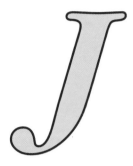

Jetsam

Anything tossed overboard or discharged, especially to lighten a boat in distress. See also *flotsam*.

Jib

A triangular *headsail*. Its *luff* usually is attached to the *forestay*, although an increasing number of sailboats have a foil with tracks into which the luff is fed in place of, or in addition to, a forestay.

Jib boom

A *spar* extending beyond the *bowsprit* to permit an additional *headsail*.

BROAD REACHING ON PORT TACK

JIBING

BROAD REACH ON STARBOARD TACK

WIND

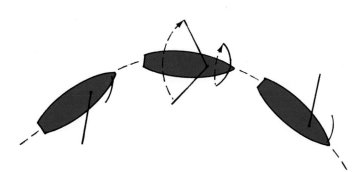

Jibe

To *tack* when sailing on a downwind *course*. The *stern* of the boat moves through the wind, and the sails fill from the *lee* side and swing over rapidly. Because of the speed of this maneuver, it is important that the boat is correctly balanced during a jibe. As with *coming about*, certain commands should be given before jibing in order to alert the crew. The command of preparation is "prepare to jibe," and that of execution is "jibe-ho."

*   *   *

One common fault while jibing is to allow the boat to round up into the wind as the *boom* swings across. This mistake has led to the *capsizing* of many a *centerboard dinghy*. By straightening the *tiller* immediately after the jibe, the *helmsman* can counteract the turning tendency of the boat and drive it forward in a straight line.

Jibe-ho

See *jibe*.

Jib-headed rig

A sailing rig with all triangular sails. More commonly called a *Marconi rig*.

This cruiser has a jib-headed rig.

Jigger

Another name for a *mizzensail* on a *ketch* or *yawl*.

Jump a halyard

A method of raising a sail in which one *crew* member pulls up slack on the *halyard* at the *mast* while another crew member *winches* or *tails* the slack in.

Jury rig

A temporary or makeshift replacement of any part of a boat's *rig* to enable it to be sailed after damage or breakage.

Kedge

A small auxiliary *anchor*. To kedge a boat is to heave the kedge forward, attached to a line, then to move the boat forward by pulling on the line to the kedge. For example, if a boat runs *aground* on a *sandbar*, the crew can heave the anchor forward and pull on it to free the boat.

This photograph shows the keel of a 12-meter being hosed down.

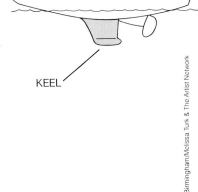

KEEL

Keel

The fixed, underwater part of a sailboat serving as ballast. All sailboats need to have a certain depth of *hull* under water in order to counteract the sideways movement created by the force of the wind on the sails (compare *centerboard* and *daggerboard*).

Keelhaul

A punishment or torture for errant sailors in which the offender is hauled from bow to stern under the boat's *keel.*

Ketch

A two-masted sailboat with a smaller *mizzen mast* stepped near the *stern* of the boat. The mizzen is forward of the point where the rudderpost intersects the *waterline.* Compare *yawl.*

Kite

Casual term for a *spinnaker.*

Knocked down

Term used to describe a boat *capsized* by a gust or *broached* so far that its *sails* and *boom* are in the water.

Knot

The speed of one nautical mile (6,080 feet or 1,842 meters) per hour; also, a means of tying a *line.*

* * *

An important skill for a new sailor to learn is tying knots that hold securely yet can be untied quickly. Rope work, a highly respected skill, has been developed over the centuries, and sailors today use many of the same knots that were employed several thousand years ago.

* * *

The type and thickness of line used obviously depends on what it is being used for. Although previously made of natural fibers such as cotton, sisal, or hemp, today synthetic fibers, such as polypropylene, polyester, and nylon, are more commonly used.

* * *

The parts of a line are as follows: The bend, or loop, is known as the *bight*; the part the bight made over is called the *standing part*; and the end of the line is called the *bitter end.*

Commonly used knots:

Bowline This knot makes a nonslip standing *eye* on the end of a *line* and is used for towing, *docking*, securing a *sheet* to a *sail*, and many other purposes. Even under tension, a bowline can be untied quickly and easily.

BOWLINE

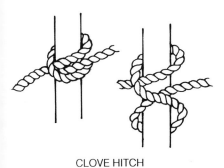

CLOVE HITCH

FIGURE EIGHT

ROUND TURN AND TWO HALF HITCHES

SQUARE KNOT

Clove hitch This knot is used as a temporary docking or mooring knot. It can come undone under sideways tension.

Figure eight Often used as a stopper knot in the end of a *line* or *sheet*, this knot is very easy to untie, even when wet.

Round turn and two half hitches This knot is most often used when tying a line (without much tension on it) to a *spar*, *rail*, or *shroud*—for example, when attaching a *fender* to the rail of a boat.

Square knot This is a strong knot that is easily tied and untied by pushing the standing parts and end toward the center of the knot.

* * *

Learning how to take care of lines is a sailor's top priority. Lines are an important part of any boat's equipment and are expensive to replace. They should be kept clean and hosed off with fresh water when possible, and should be coiled carefully and hung to dry before stowing.

Knotmeter _____
An instrument for measuring a boat's speed.

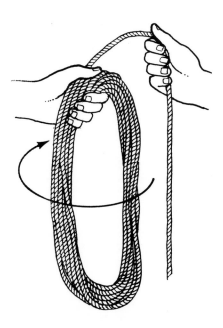

COMPLETED COIL

Labor
To pitch or roll in heavy seas.

Lacing
Line used to secure the sail to a *spar*, it passes through eyeholes located in the sail.

Lagoon
A shallow sound enclosed, or mostly enclosed, by coral islands, atolls, or reefs.

Land breeze
An offshore night breeze blowing from the cool land to the warm sea.

Landfall
When land is first sighted.

A land breeze is often felt as the sun sets.

The leading edge, or luff, of the headsail is attached to the headstay.

© Albert B. Fisk/FPG International

Lanyard_____

A short piece of lightweight line fastened to an object such as a knife, small tool, or pail, for the purpose of securing it.

Lash_____

To secure an object with a line.

Lateen_____

An ancient rig featuring a narrow triangular sail set on a very long *yard*. The rig today is restricted to the relatively calm water found in certain areas of Africa and the Middle East.

Latitude_____

Distance north or south of the equator, measured in degrees.

Launch_____

A small boat used to ferry people back and forth between moored boats or land.

Lay_____

To *fetch* a mark—to make the intended course without changing *tack*.

Layline_____

The *close-hauled* course to a windward mark. Also, the fastest downwind sailing angle to a *leeward* mark.

Lay up_____

To store a boat during the winter months. Also, to take a boat out of commission.

Lazarette_____

A small compartment in the *stern* used for storage.

Lazy guy_____

See *spinnaker*.

Lead line_____

The traditional measure of depth. Modern lead lines are usually calibrated in feet or *fathoms*. The bottom of the lead has a shallow depression, which, when filled with grease or wax, brings up a sample of the seabed.

Leading edge_____

Forward part of a sail or *keel*.

Leading wind_____

A *fair wind*.

League_____

Antiquated nautical distance measurement, equal to three nautical miles.

Lee_____

The area to *leeward*. To be in the lee of an object is to be sheltered by it.

Lee boards_____

Boards fitted to the outside of a bunk to prevent the occupant from falling out. Also, boards stretched vertically to a boat's *hull* to prevent *leeway*.

Lee bow

In racing, an advantageous tactical position ahead and to *leeward* of another close-hauled boat. The *windward* boat sails in a *headed* air flow, and the leeward boat sails in a *lifted* and accelerated flow.

Leech

The trailing, unattached edge of a triangular sail.

Lee helm

The designed tendency of a boat to head away from the wind if the *helm* is left unattended.

Lee tide

Tidal current running with the wind.

Leeward (*pronounced loo'ard*)

The direction to which the wind is blowing; opposite of *windward*.

The curved leech of the mainsail is reinforced with battens.

Leeway

The sideways motion of a boat to *leeward* caused by wind and sea action.

Length overall (LOA)

The total length of a boat, from *bow* to *stern*, not including any *bowsprit*.

Lifeline

A *line* rigged around an open *deck* for the safety of the *crew*.

Life preserver

Buoyant device to keep a person in the water afloat.

Lift

A wind shift away from the *bow*, which permits a *close-hauled* boat to *head up*.

Line

Nautical term for rope.

List

When a boat leans at any angle caused by weight on board rather than the pressure of wind or waves.

© Ulf Sjostedt/FPG International

Above: Lifelines, supported by stanchions, provide security for the crew on deck.

Right: The life buoy shown here is designed to support a human body in the water.

© Billy Black/Envision

Lloyd's Register of Shipping

The first and largest ship classification organization worldwide. Formed in 1760, this society's goal was the establishment of construction and maintenance standards for merchant ships. The register book, published annually, lists all merchant ships of fleets, shipbuilders, and docks. Registers of British and American yachts are also published annually.

Load waterline (LWL)

The straight-line distance from the point where the *bow* emerges from the water to the point where the *stern* emerges; the waterline length.

Log

An electronic or mechanical instrument fixed to a boat's *keel* to measure its speed through the water.

The helmsman and crew shown here are wearing standard life jackets. In this type of boat, this kind of buoyancy aid is the best choice.

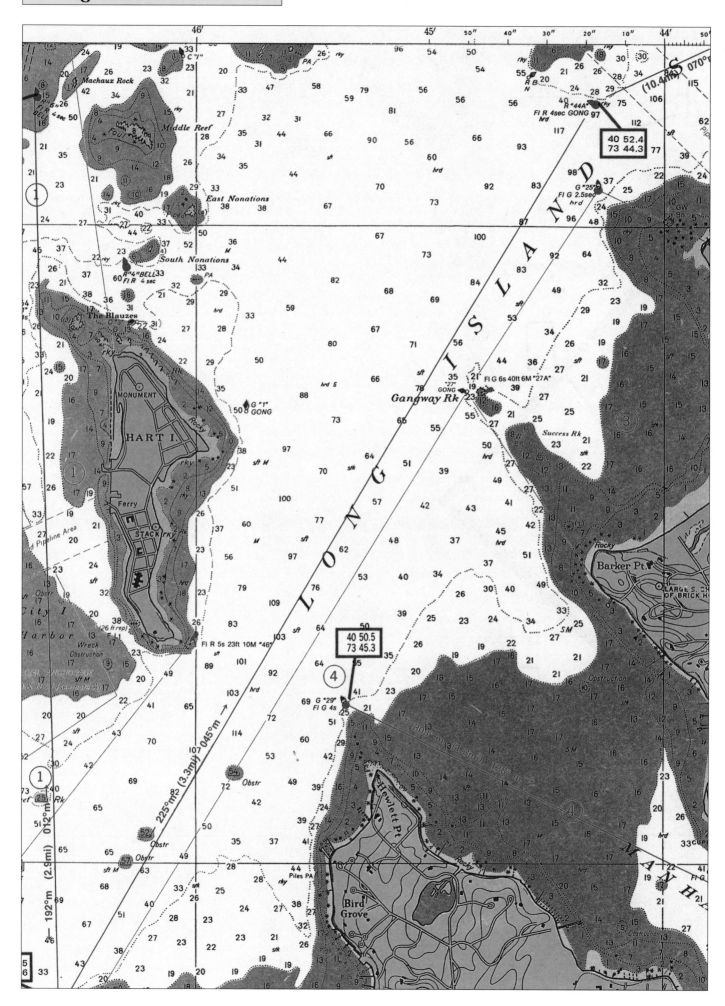

Log book

Boat's journal containing a daily record of course sailed, distance covered, weather conditions, and other important events that occur on board. As with the daily maintenance required on a pleasure cruise, keeping a log seems at first tedious and unnecessary. However, the log provides excellent information for planning future cruises.

Longitude

A measurement of distance expressed in degrees east or west from the Greenwich meridian.

Loose

To *unfurl* a sail.

Loose cover

In racing, a defensive controlling position ahead of a boat (or boats) in which the lead boat does not aerodynamically affect the following boat(s). Compare *tight cover*.

Loran

An electronic long-range navigation system that uses shore-based radio transmitters and shipboard receivers to allow sailors to determine their position. Loran was originally developed during World War II for military operations; today there are more than fifty stations operating for the U.S. and Canadian Atlantic and Pacific coasts, the upper North Atlantic Ocean, the Mediterranean, parts of the North Pacific west of Hawaii and south of Japan, and off the coast of Saudi Arabia.

* * *

Loran transmitters all operate on 100 kHz in chains of a master station and several secondary stations. The stations that form a chain are spread out to provide signal coverage over a wide coastal area. Chains are identified by their individual pulse group repetition intervals (GRIs)— the time, measured in microseconds, between transmissions of the master signal. The difference in the time of arrival at the shipboard receiver of pulse groups from the master and secondary stations is measured electronically and used to find a line of position (LOP). Using two or more master-secondary pairs of signals yields the same amount of LOPs, and therefore determines a Loran *fix*.

Low

An area of low barometric pressure, generally accompanied by bad weather and high winds.

Courtesy King Marine Electronics, Inc.

Opposite page: **The fine black lines on a nautical chart denote meridians of longitude and parallels of latitude.**

Above: **Loran.**

© Christopher Bain

The lugsail is said to be a Western adaptation of the short-boomed Chinese lugsail.

Luff

The forward, or _leading_, _edge_ of a sail. To _luff up_ is to bring a boat's _bow_ closer to the wind until the leech of the _sail_ flaps.

Luff up

To point a boat's _bow_ into the wind. In racing, the tactical maneuver of a leeward boat forcing a windward boat to sail closer to the wind.

Lugsail

A four-sided sail set for small boats that resembles a _gaff sail_. It was used as early as the seventeenth century in Europe and it is believed to have been adapted from a short-boomed Chinese sailing vessel.

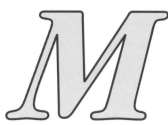

Mainsail (pronounced mains'l)

The principal sail on a boat, which is trimmed to drive the boat in a given direction. The triangular _Marconi_ mainsail, from which the _rig_ derives its name, superseded the four-sided _gaff_ sail early in the twentieth century.

Make fast

To secure a _line_.

Make sail

To set sail.

Marconi rig

See *sailboat rig*.

Maritime

Pertaining to the sea.

Mark

Markings on a lead line that show depth visually or by feel. Strips of leather or brightly colored bunting are among the materials used as marks. Also, any buoy or object specified in racing instructions that a boat must round or pass on a required side.

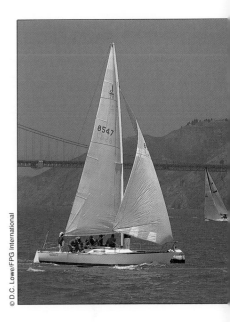

Above: A J-29 rounding a mark.

Left: The principal sail of a sailing vessel is the mainsail.

© Allan Weitz

Marlinespike

A pointed metal or wooden spike used for opening up strands of line when *splicing*.

Mast

A vertical *spar* to which *sails* are attached. The mast is usually secured in a vertical position by wires called *shrouds*, which are affixed to the side *decks* and the *forestay*, which attaches to the *bow*. See *rigging*.

Mast step

Frame or slot to secure lower end, or butt, of the *mast*.

Masthead

The top of the mast.

Masthead fly

A light weather vane at the top of the mast; also called a *wind indicator*.

Masthead light

See *running lights*.

Masthead sloop

A *sloop* on which the *forestay* reaches to the *masthead*.

Mayday

International distress signal, from the French *m'aidez*, meaning "Help me."

Mean low water

The average depth at low tide.

Median

In an *oscillating shift* pattern, the direction of the wind midway between the most *veered* and most *backed* winds.

Opposite page: The masts of most modern yachts and racing dinghies are made from aluminum, and are shaped aerodynamically to reduce windage and create lift.

Above: The bottom of the mast is fitted into a socket called a mast step.

Meridian

An imaginary circle that passes through the north and south poles and cuts the equator at right angles. Lines of *longitude* are all meridians.

Messenger

A light line used to lead over a heavier rope or cable.

Midships, amidships

In the middle part of a boat.

Mizzenmast

The aftermost mast on a *yawl* or *ketch*.

Mizzen sail

Sail set from mizzenmast.

Mizzen staysail

A triangular *headsail* bent to a temporary *stay* from the *mizzenmast* to the deck.

Moor

To fasten a boat to a *mooring*.

Mooring

A permanent *anchorage*, usually consisting of an *anchor* or a heavy weight, a length of chain, and a *buoy* that often has a pennant attached.

Opposite page: **Cruiser reaching under mainsail and mizzen.**

Below: **The moorings in this photograph are spaced to ensure that the boats attached to them won't hit one another.**

Multihull

Generic term for any boat with more than one hull, including the *catamaran* (two hulls), the *trimaran* (main hull, with floats on either side), and the outrigger (main hull and a smaller side float).

This catamaran, one type of multihull, is sailing fast downwind.

Nautical Almanac

An annual guide that contains tidal and astronomical information for sailors. It is published by the U.S. Naval Observatory and can be obtained from the Superintendent of Documents, U.S. Government Printing Office, Washington, D.C. 20402.

Nautical mile

The unit of distance most commonly used in navigation, measured as one minute of *latitude*, or 6,076.1155 feet (1,841.2471 meters).

Navigable

Describes water that is deep enough to allow a craft passage.

Navigation

The science of determining a boat's position and conducting it safely to a destination by using charts, instruments, and/or the stars.

Neap tide

The tide which occurs about two days after the first and last quarters of the moon. It is characterized by the lowest high water and the highest low water; opposite of *spring tide*.

Near

Close to the wind.

New York Yacht Club

Organized in 1844, this was the first yacht club on the east coast of the United States. Quartered in New York City, the club boasts fine collections of model ships and nineteenth-century silver yachting trophies.

Nimbostratus

See *clouds*.

No-go zone

The area about 45° on either side of the wind into which a boat cannot sail without *coming about*.

O

Oakum

Old, tarred strands made from worn hemp *lines*, used for caulking between the planks of wooden boats.

Observed position

A boat's position plotted on a *chart* through the observation of landmarks, as opposed to *dead reckoning*.

Offshore breeze

A *land breeze*. Sometimes bugs get blown off land and alight on an anchored vessel, something to be taken into account when selecting an anchorage.

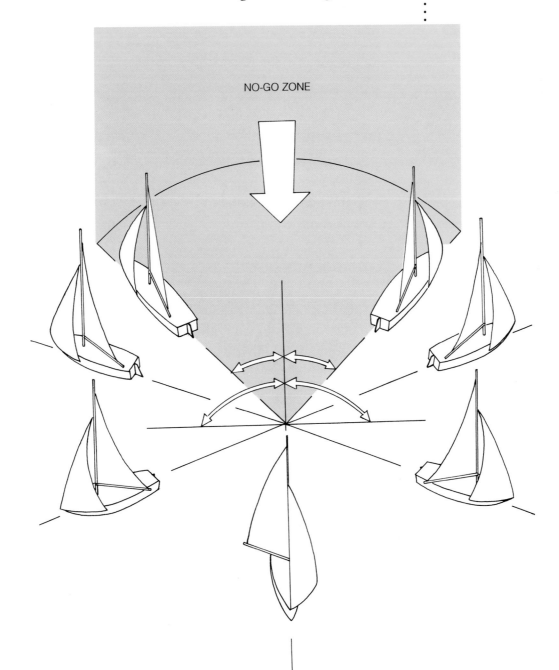

NO-GO ZONE

Right: A fleet of Lasers, a popular one-design, skims across the water before the start of a race.

Opposite page: The outhaul attaches the clew of the mainsail to the end of the boom.

© Allan Weitz

Off the wind

Sailing *downwind* with the *sheets eased*. Sailing as close to the wind as possible is to be "on the wind."

One-design

Sailboats built to uniform specifications and measurements, and equipped with the same rigging in accordance with class guidelines. Most one-design classes allow maximum and minimum measurements, or tolerances, and variations in fittings.

Oscillating shift

A wind-shift pattern that varies between a *veered* and *backed* limit over a regular period of oscillation. These shifts often occur with *offshore winds* and *cumulus* clouds.

Outhaul

The *line* or wire that attaches the *clew* of the *mainsail* to the outboard end of the *boom*. Its function is to adjust the tension along the *foot* of the sail: taut, for a flatter sail, when sailing *upwind* or on a breezy day; loose, for a fuller sail, when sailing *downwind* or on a calm day.

Out point

To sail closer to the wind than another boat.

Overfall

When waves break suddenly over a reef, shoal, or where two currents meet.

Overhang

The part or parts of a boat that extend beyond the waterline at the *bow* or *stern*.

Overstand

A racing term that describes sailing past the *layline* to a *mark*. This is a basic tactical error that wastes distance.

Painter

A *bowline*.

Palm

A sailmaker's thimble. It is strapped to the palm of the hand when pushing a needle through the sailcloth.

Parallel rules

A traditional plotting instrument used in *navigation*, it is a pair of straight edges fastened together so that the distance between them may be changed while they remain parallel and their direction remains the same.

Parrel

A *fitting*, usually made of *shock cord*, *line*, or wire, used to hold a *spar* to the *mast*. Spars on *square-rigged* ships are held to the mast by parrels so that they swing freely.

Pass

To take securing wraps with a lashing or *line*.

Passage

A sailing voyage from one *port* to another.

Pay off

To turn the *bow* away from the wind, or to *leeward*.

Pay out

To let out a *line* or cable so that it runs freely.

Peak

The upper corner of a four-sided sail; usually associated with a *gaff* sail.

Pelorus

A portable navigational instrument used for taking *bearings* in any direction relative to a boat's *heading*. It consists of a sighting device mounted on a graduated *compass card* called a pelorus card, about which is fixed a ring calibrated in degrees.

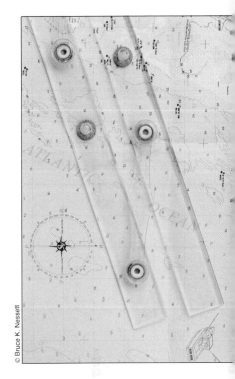

© Bruce K. Nessett

Opposite page: **The upper aft corner of the gaff-rigged sail is called the peak.**

Above: **Parallel rules on a chart.**

Pennant

A long, narrow flag often used for yacht club or racing class designations.

Permanent backstay

A *backstay* that clears the *boom*. Compare *running backstay*.

Persistent shift

A steady wind shift in one direction, usually to the right in the northern hemisphere. These shifts may occur with onshore breezes.

Pier

A structure, usually wooden, built out over the water and used by boats to land. Same as a *jetty* or *wharf*.

Pilings

Thick posts or timbers driven into the seabed that project above the water, used to support or *moor* a *dock* or *pier*.

Pilot

A person licensed to navigate vessels through *channels* and in and out of *port*.

© Allan Weitz

***Top:* Pitch is a boat's fore-and-aft motion.**

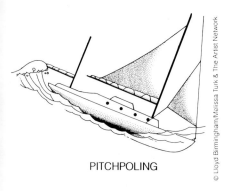

© Lloyd Birmingham/Melissa Turk & The Artist Network

PITCHPOLING

***Above:* The most spectacular form of capsize, called pitchpoling, occurs when the bow digs into a wave and the boat flips stern-over-bow.**

Piloting (pilotage)

The technique of directing a vessel by referring to landmarks, navigational aids such as lighthouses and *buoys*, soundings, and electronic navigational systems. Good piloting requires constant vigilance, mental alertness, and experience since there is often little opportunity to correct errors.

Pinch

To sail too close to the wind, above a *close-hauled* position. Optional speed is sacrificed for a higher heading. Pinching may be caused by an inattentive or overanxious *helmsman*.

Pinnance

A boat or vessel that can be sailed or rowed; often used as a *tender*.

Pintle

A metal pin on a removable *rudder* that inserts into a *gudgeon* on a boat's *stern*.

Pitch

Boiled-tar residue, used for caulking wooden boats. Also, the motion of a boat's bow plunging forward and downward into the trough of a wave.

Pitchpole

The *stern*-over-*bow* somersault of a boat that can occur in high seas.

© Patrick Walmsley/Envision

Plain sailing

Simple sailing, without impediment.

Plane

This action depends on the hull design and weight of the boat. Forward speed creates hydrodynamic lift, thus reducing friction and increasing speed.

Planing hull

A hull design that achieves most of its underway load-carrying ability by the dynamic action of its bottom and the top of the water over which it is moving.

Planking

The covering of the ribs of a vessel's *hull* with planks during construction.

Plot

To mark *courses* and *bearings* on a *chart*.

This dinghy is planing fast on a reach, the helmsman in the correct position.

Point

A compass is divided into thirty-two points, with a point equal to 11.25 degrees. The cardinal points of North, South, East, and West are divided by half-cardinal points, North East, South East, South West, and North West. The system of points allows for directions to be expressed through a circle centered on the *helmsman's* boat. The point system is somewhat analogous to the clock system of directions, in which 12 o'clock is dead ahead, 3 o'clock is on the starboard beam, 6 o'clock is dead astern, 9 o'clock is on the port beam. Geographically, a point is a projection of land from a coastline.

Point high

To sail very close to the wind.

Points of sail

Terms that describe the different angles from the wind on which a boat may sail. They are as follows:

Close-hauled is sailing as close to the wind as possible without *luffing*. About 45° from the wind is average, although some boats can *point higher*.

Close reach is any *heading* between close-hauled and a *beam reach*. The wind should be forward of *abeam*.

Beam reach is sailing at an angle of 90° from the wind.

Broad reach is any heading between a *beam reach* and a *run*.

Run is sailing with the wind pushing the boat from behind, at an angle of about 180° from the wind.

Polaris

The North Star, also known as the Pole Star. It indicates north within a couple of degrees.

Pole lift

See *topping lift*.

Poop

An archaic term for the after section of a vessel. A poop deck is a deck above the upper deck *abaft* the *mizzenmast*, commonly seen in sixteenth-century vessels. A craft is pooped when a wave breaks over its stern.

Port

The left side of a boat, looking toward the *bow;* opposite of *starboard.* Also, a place where vessels may discharge or take on their passengers or cargoes.

Port tack

A boat is on port tack when the breeze is blowing over its *port* side.

Porthole

A window in a boat's side.

Pram

A small rectangular *dinghy,* often used as a tender.

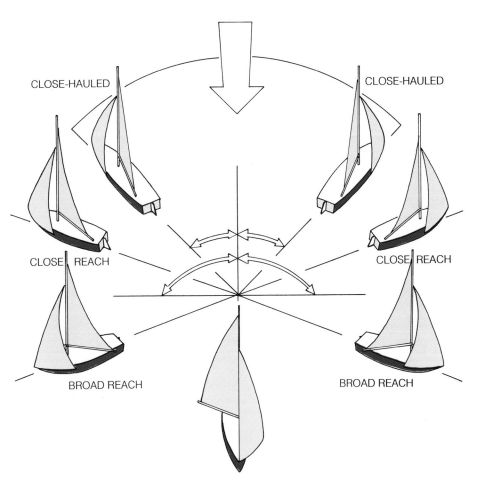

WIND

CLOSE-HAULED

CLOSE-HAULED

CLOSE REACH

CLOSE REACH

BROAD REACH

BROAD REACH

RUN

This small dinghy is on a port tack.

© Steve Arcella

© Trefethen/FPG International

The strong steel frame at the bow is called a pulpit. Lifelines run from the pulpit back to the cockpit to provide security for the crew while on deck.

The sailboat is the privileged vessel over the power boat.

Prevailing wind

The usual wind direction for a particular season.

Preventer

An additional *line* set up to limit excess movement in the *boom*, thus preventing an accidental *jibe*.

Privileged

A privileged boat is allowed to hold its speed and course when another boat approaches.

Propeller

An engine-driven rotating screw, which pushes a boat through the sea. The propeller's thrust is achieved by drawing water from *ahead* and pushing it *astern*.

Protest flag

A red flag raised during a race when a competitor believes it has been fouled by another boat.

Puff

Visible on the water as dark ripples darting across the surface. A *helmsman* should *head up* in puffs. This maintains the original angle of the wind to the sails because the *apparent wind* comes *aft* in puffs.

Pulpit

A guardrail at the *bow* or *stern*. Also known as a pushpit.

Punt

A flat-bottomed, rectangular boat, usually propelled by a pole.

Purchase

The leverage given by any mechanical device; used to raise or move an object or trim a *sheet*.

Quarters

Sleeping and living area on a vessel. It is not difficult to discover the origin of today's "close quarters," given the cramped sleeping berths on ships.

Quay

Wharf used for loading and unloading cargo.

Quarter

There are four quarters on a boat, two *fore* and two *aft*, midway between the *beam* and the *stern*.

*   *   *

Also, a steady wind from a particular direction is said to be in that direction's quarter. For example, the wind is in the northeast quarter if it has been blowing from that direction for some time.

Quarter berth

A *berth* or bunk that is located under the side of the *cockpit*.

Race

An area characterized by a strong, confused, fast-moving current, usually caused by a narrow channel, uneven sea bottom, or tidal interaction.

Race committee

The organizing authority who arranges, conducts, and judges a sailboat race or a *regatta*.

Radar

A detecting device that focuses a strong scanning beam of ultrahigh-frequency radio waves. Through the reception and timing of the sound waves, it can establish distance and direction of motion of anything in the beam's path.

Radio direction finder (RDF)

A portable navigational instrument that enables a navigator to take a *bearing* on a signal transmitted from a marine radio beacon and cross it with bearings from other beacons to *fix* a boat's position. An RDF cannot determine distance from a beacon, and many sailors today use *Loran,* which is a more expensive aid to navigation, but is more reliable.

Rail

The outer edge of the *deck.*

Raise a light

The crew or skipper are said to have raised a light when a light becomes visible just as one raises a cape or point when such a landmark comes into view.

Rake

The angle of a ship's *mast* compared to a line perpendicular to the *deck.* Where that angle is wide, the boat is apt to have an excessive *lee* or *weather helm,* although this depends on where the foot of the mast is located.

These rope steps, called ratlines, are used by crew working aloft in square-rigged ships.

Courtesy Island Packet Yachts

The first and easiest point of sail for the novice to learn is the beam reach.

Range

The difference in the water's depth between high and low tide.

Range lights

Vertical white lights indicating a vessel's heading in perspective to a channel entrance.

Ranges

Pairs of lit or unlit fixed markers showing the center line of a channel when they are observed in a straight line. They are called leading marks when they are at the mouth of a harbor or river and are normally marked on charts.

Rating

A handicapping formula using time allowances and finishing order applied to racing boats of different sizes and classes so that they can race together on a handicap basis.

Ratlines

Small lines tied across the *shrouds* to form ladders or steps.

Reach

To sail with the wind *abeam*. See *Points of sail*.

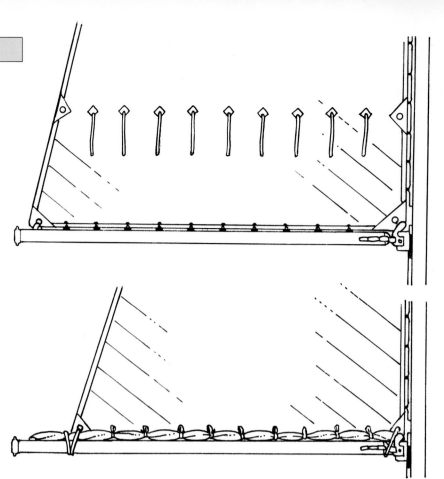

A mainsail before and after being reefed.

Reaching jib or reacher

A jib often used by racers on some classes of boats when on a *broad reach*. It is larger and lighter than a working jib.

"Ready about"

A command to stand by in preparation for *coming about* onto the opposite *track*.

Reckoning

See *dead reckoning*.

Reef

To reduce the *mainsail* area by partially lowering the sail and securing the unused portion; usually a preparation for an approaching storm or high winds. A jiffy reef system enables a crew to accomplish a reef quickly by utilizing *blocks* and *lines*. A single person in a boat can use a fisherman's reef, which entails pulling the *traveler* all the way up to *windward*. The resulting twist in the *mainsail* spills wind out of the sail, thus depowering the boat.

Reef points

Short pieces of *line* hung from the *eyes* in the reef band of a sail for securing the reefed portion of the sail. They are usually tied with a *square knot*, which unties easily.

Reeve

To pass the end of a *line* through a hole. For example, to reeve a *tackle* is to lead a line through its *blocks*.

Regatta

Originally a term for gondola races in Venice, today a regatta is any organized series of sailing or rowing races.

Registry

Ship's papers that show the ownership and national registration.

This crew member is reeving a tackle.

View of rigging aloft.

Ride

To lie smoothly at anchor. Also, to ride out a storm is to wait for the gale to blow over.

Rig

See *sailboat rig.*

Rigging

All the lines and wires used aboard a sailboat to keep the mast up and work the sails. There are two categories—running rigging and standing rigging.

* * *

Running rigging is the generic term for *halyards*, which hoist and lower the sails, and *sheets*, which are the *lines* attached to the sails so that they may be trimmed. Halyards and sheets take the name of the sail to which they are attached; for example, main sheet, jib halyard.

* * *

Standing rigging comprises the wires that hold up the mast. *Stays* prevent the mast from falling over the *bow* or *stern*. The stay leading forward from the mast to the bow is called the headstay, forestay, or jibstay. The one leading from the top of the mast to the deck in the middle of the stern is called the backstay.

* * *

Shrouds are the wires that prevent the mast from toppling sideways. They lead up to attachment points on the mast, and since the angle they make is more acute than that of the stays, the shrouds that lead highest on the mast run through struts on either side of the mast called *spreaders.* These widen the angle the shrouds make with the mast, resulting in stronger support for the top section of the mast.

Right

To return to an upright position, as in righting a *capsized* boat.

Right of way

The legal authority for one boat to hold its course while another boat gives way.

Rip

An area of water made rough and treacherous by the meeting of opposing tides or currents.

Roach

The gently curved portion of the *leech* of a sail.

Roaring forties

The stormy areas of ocean between the fortieth and fiftieth degrees of latitude, north or south.

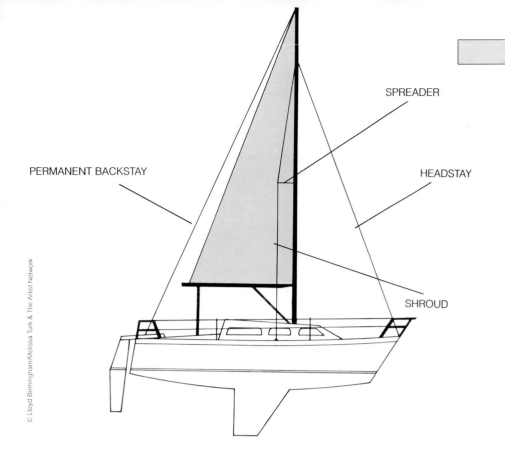

SPREADER

PERMANENT BACKSTAY

HEADSTAY

SHROUD

The outwardly curving roach of this mainsail is evident here.

© Tim Gibson/Envision

Technically, rope becomes line on board a sailing vessel.

Roll _____
Side-to-side motion of a vessel.

Roller reef _____
Reef made by mechanical means. The sail is rolled around a *boom* or *stay*.

Rope _____
Strands of fiber or wire braided or twisted together. Ropes used in operation of a sailboat are called *lines*. Ropes can be made from natural or synthetic fibers or from wire. Ropes of any making should be rinsed after use and protected from salt water and dust. A rope should be coiled in the same direction as the strands are twisted. Care must also be taken to prevent the ends from fraying.

Rudder _____
A movable underwater plate attached to the *stern* or beneath the *hull*, used for steering. It both initiates changes in direction and provides resistance to the sideways motion of a boat caused by wind and waves. The rudder is adjusted by the *tiller* or steering wheel.

Rules of the Road _____
International traffic regulations for vessels of all sizes both on the ocean and in other waters. Other rules, speed limits and pilot rules, for example, are laid down by the Coast Guard and local authorities.

Run _____
See *points of sail*.

Running backstay

A movable backstay, which is trimmed as part of the running rigging. A boat with running backstays will have a pair, usually with one rigged on each side of a boat, and, when sailing, only the *windward* one is tensioned.

Running lights

The lights carried from dusk to dawn aboard a vessel; required by law. Different combinations of lights show whether a boat is under motor or sail, at anchor, or under tow.

© Ronald E. Partis/Envision

© Christopher Bain

Left: The rudder must be adjusted constantly by using the tiller when a boat is being sailed.

Above: The leeward running backstay should always be eased.

Safety harness_____

A harness used to attach a crew member to a boat in rough weather.

Sailboat rig_____

The manner in which a boat's *mast, sails,* and *spars* are arranged. Sailboats fall into one of two categories depending on how many masts and their location.

*　　*　　*

Sailboats with one mast are either *sloops, cutters,* or *catboats.*
A sloop has two sails, a *headsail* forward of a *mainsail.* The mast in a cutter must be more than two-fifths of the *waterline* length *aft* of the point where the *bow* emerges from the water. A catboat does not carry a *jib,* and the mast is closer to the bow.

*　　*　　*

Sailboats with two masts are either *ketches, yawls,* or *schooners.*
In ketches and yawls the smaller mast, called the *mizzenmast,* is aft of the larger. In a *ketch* the mizzen is forward of the point where the rudderpost intersects the waterline. In a yawl the mizzen is aft of this point. If the forward mast is the same size or smaller than the aftermast on a double-masted boat, then it is called a schooner. Schooners can have three, four, or even more masts.

*　　*　　*

There are also two classifications of sail plans. A *Marconi-rigged* (also called Bermuda) sail is a triangular sail rigged fore and aft. Most small single-masted boats today are Marconi-rigged, as the sails are efficient and simple to handle. A *gaff-rigged* mainsail is a four-sided, fore-and-aft rigged sail that is essentially rectangular. With the addition of a fourth side, or *head,* the gaff-rigged main requires an additional *spar* called a *gaff* to aid in hoisting and lowering the sail. This procedure calls for an additional *halyard* as well. Gaff-rigged boats have been in use centuries longer than Marconi-rigged boats, but they are not commonly seen today. One advantage to a gaff-rigged main is that it is easy to *reef* in a gale, but it is not as efficient as a Marconi-rigged main, and the two halyards and a spar make it more complicated to handle.

SLOOP

CAT BOAT

CUTTER

KETCH

YAWL

SCHOONER

Sails

Modern sails are most often made of Dacron™ or nylon, although Mylar™ and Kevlar™ are also used. Sails are the driving force of a boat. When set at the correct angle to the wind, they convert the force of the wind into *heeling* and forward impulsion.

*   *   *

Most sailboats have two sails (see *rig*): one forward of the *mast* and the other *aft*, and they must be properly balanced. The *mainsail* and the *jib* propel the boat forward; a *spinnaker* is often used when sailing *downwind* to increase speed.

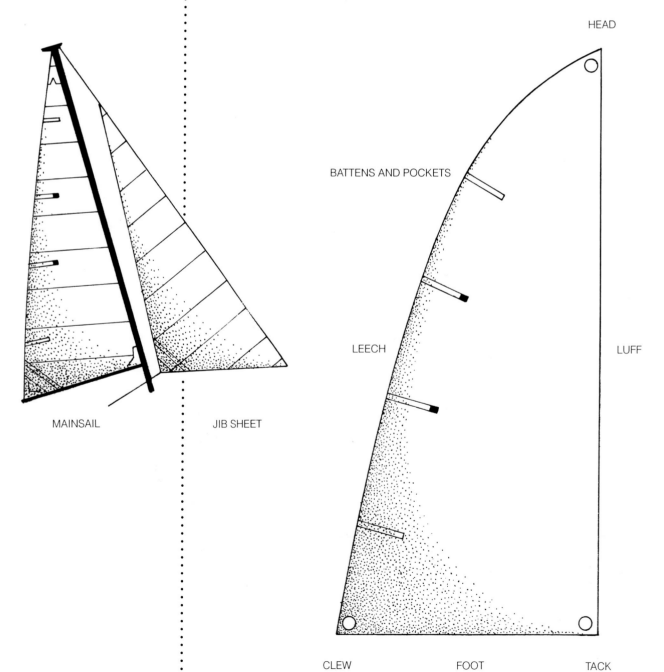

MAINSAIL   JIB SHEET

HEAD

BATTENS AND POCKETS

LEECH   LUFF

CLEW   FOOT   TACK

WORKING SAILS

STORM SAILS

MAINSAIL

MIZZEN

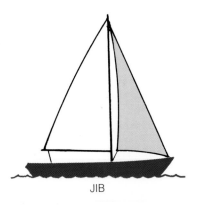

JIB

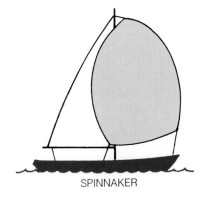

SPINNAKER

Sail high

To sail as close to the wind as possible.

Sail track

A metal strip fitted along the length of a *mast* or *boom* into which a sail is inserted by *lugs* attached to its edge.

Salvage

Reward for saving a ship or its cargo from danger. Also, the act of saving a ship or its cargo.

Sampson post

A sturdy metal or wooden post to which lines can be made fast.

Sandbar

A ridge of sand built up by *currents*.

Satellite navigation (SATNAV)

More precisely known as the Navy Navigational Satellite System, SATNAV consists of several satellites that orbit the earth and send transmissions to shipboard receivers, which then calculate and display the vessel's position.

* * *

In the next few years a new satellite system, the Global Position System (GPS), will be implemented. This system will comprise more than twenty satellites in twelve-hour orbits, thus permitting information from multiple satellites to be calculated simultaneously.

Scandalize

To temporarily shorten the sails in a *gaff-rigged* ship by hauling up the *tack* and lowering the *peak*.

Schooner

A double-masted ship where the forward *mast* is the same size as, or smaller than, the aftermast. Schooners can have three, four, or even more masts.

Scope

The ratio of anchor line or chain to the depth of water beneath the keel. Under favorable conditions a minimum scope is about 5:1 or 6:1. In rough conditions it might be necessary to increase the scope.

Scow

A flat-bottomed racing boat with square ends, fitted with dual *centerboards* and dual *rudders*.

Scud

To *run* before the wind in a gale, often with a *reefed mainsail* or *bare poles*.

© Christopher Bain

Opposite page: **Unlike other sails, the spinnaker isn't fastened along the luff to a boom or stay.**

Above: **Schooner.**

Scuttle

To put holes in a ship's bottom to make it sink.

Sea anchor

A *drogue* used as a floating *anchor* to aid a boat in *riding* out a storm.

Sea breeze

An onshore breeze flowing from cool water to sun-warmed land, it occurs in the summer months on bright sunny days.

Scull

To propel a small boat forward with a single oar over the stern in a movement that resembles the action of a fish's tail. Also, in racing, a repeated, forceful movement of the helm, which is against the yacht-racing rules.

Scupper

A drain or opening through the *rail*, *gunwale*, or *planking* that allows water taken on in rough seas to flow overboard.

Sea cock

A valve fitted onto an underwater drain on a boat.

Sea mile

A *nautical mile*.

Sea room

Sufficient space from the shore to permit unrestricted maneuvers.

Seize

To fasten together with a lashing of small *line* or yarn.

Set

Effect of a tidal *current* on a boat. Also, to hoist sails.

Set a course

To steer a boat.

Sextant

A navigation instrument used to measure the altitude of celestial bodies, thus determining the position of a boat. A sextant is capable of great accuracy and is considered the precision instrument for celestial navigation.

Shackle

A U-shaped metal fastener with a pin or snap closing. Its many uses include connecting the anchor to the chain and the chain to the anchor line, securing *stays* and attaching *halyards* to *sails*.

Sheave (*pronounced shiv*)

The wheel in a *block*.

Sailor using a sextant, which measures vertical and horizontal angles at sea.

© Joe Viesti/Viesti Associates, Inc.

Sheer

The curve of the deck of a boat as viewed from the side. Also, to alter course rapidly. To sheer off is to bear away.

Sheerpole

A metal rod secured horizontally at the foot of a mast's *standing rigging* that keeps the *shrouds* from untwisting.

Sheet

See *rigging*.

Ship

A power-driven vessel that carries passengers or cargo and is capable of long seagoing voyages; traditionally, a sailing vessel *square-rigged* on three or more masts. Also, to take water over the *gunwales,* as in a heavy sea.

Shoal

An area of water that is shallow. Also, a *sandbar* that makes the water shallow.

Shock cord

A type of strong elasticized line.

Shorthanded

Short of the regular or required number of crew members.

Shroud

See *rigging*.

Single up

To cast off all lines except one at each position.

Skeg

A projecting part of the underwater surface of a boat.

Above: **Two kinds of ships are shown above: an ocean liner and a schooner.**

Opposite page: **View of the sheer, or curve, of a boat's deck.**

Above: **Boats docked in slips at a marina.**

Slack _____

Limp part of a sail or line. Also, to ease off a line.

Slack tide _____

A brief period when the tide turns and there is no tidal movement either way.

Slat _____

To flap loudly, as loose *halyards* against a *mast*.

Slip _____

A *berth* at a *dock* where a boat may be *made fast*.

Sloop _____

A single-masted sailboat that has two sails, a *headsail* forward of a *mainsail*.

Slot effect _____

The bending and funneling of air behind the *mainsail* through the "slot" between the *mainsail* and the *jib*. This increases the speed of the air on the *lee* side of the main, thus increasing its suction and efficiency (see *Bernoulli's principle*).

Sounding _____

The measurement of water depth beneath a boat. See *lead line*.

Southern Ocean Racing Conference (SORC) _____

A prestigious offshore racing series, comparable in stature to Britain's Admiral's Cup. This annual event was first organized in 1941.

Sou'wester

A gale blowing from the southwest. Also, a canvas or oilcloth hat with a long flap on the back, traditionally worn at sea in stormy weather.

Spanker

The fore-and-aft rigged sail on the aftermast of a *square-rigged* vessel. Also, the aftermast and its sail on a *schooner* with four or more *masts*.

Spar

A generic term for *masts*, *booms*, *bowsprits*, and *gaffs*.

Spill the wind

To take the wind out of a sail by *easing* the sheet so that the sail swings to a position where it can't hold the wind.

Above: **The mast and boom shown here are both spars.**

Left: **A sloop rig is the most common rig seen on modern boats.**

© Christopher Bain

Spinnaker

An additional, three-cornered sail that acts as a large parachute, pulling a boat downwind. Made of lightweight cloth, usually nylon, a spinnaker adds extra sail area to the total sail plan of a boat, thus increasing boat speed when it is set. Spinnakers are usually referred to by the weight per square yard of the material used, such as 3/4 ounce, and by the composition of the sail panels, such as star cut or radial cut.

* * *

The spinnaker is raised by the spinnaker *halyard*. One *clew* is attached to a line (called the spinnaker *guy)* held in place by a spinnaker pole, which attaches to the mast and is always set to *windward*, opposite the main *boom*. The outboard end of the pole is clipped to the windward spinnaker *sheet*, or afterguy. Where double sheets and guys are used so that there is a sheet and guy on each side of the boat, the guy not in use is called the lazy guy. The free clew has a sheet attached to it, just like any other sail.

Splicing

A method of joining *lines* or lines and wires by separating the strands and weaving them together.

Spreaders

Metal or wooden struts attached horizontally on either side of the upper section of a *mast*. They widen the angle of the *shrouds* with the mast, thus providing better support for the top of the mast.

Opposite page: **A perfectly set spinnaker on an Etchells 22 sailing on a close reach.**

Above: **Spreaders.**

The square rig is very old, said to have first been made by the Scandinavians around the tenth century A.D.

Spring

To bend, warp, or strain to the point of cracking, as in springing a *mast*. Also, to open a seam in a boat's hull, thus springing a leak.

Spring tide

The tide which occurs at or near the full and new moons. It is characterized by the highest high tides and the lowest low tides. Opposite of *neap tide*.

Spritsail

A four-sided, *fore-and-aft-sail* set on a long *spar* called a sprit. Spritsails on the *mizzen* of *square-rigged* ships became more-or-less antiquated with the invention of the *gaff* sail in the late seventeenth century.

Spyglass

A small hand telescope.

Square-rigged

Setting sails so that they hang *athwart* a ship. Hung on *yards*, the sails are four-sided. Square-rigged vessels, well-suited to sailing *downwind*, traveled the oceans by using the steady trade winds. See also *Tall ships*.

Stanchion

An upright metal post used to support *lifelines* or a guardrail.

Standing part

The part of a *knot* that the *bight* is made over.

Standing rigging

See *rigging*.

Starboard *(pronounced star'bd)* _____

The right side of a boat, looking toward the *bow*; opposite of *port*.

Starboard tack _____

A boat is on starboard *tack* when the breeze is blowing from its starboard side to its port side.

Stay _____

See *rigging*.

Staysail _____

A triangular sail set *aft* of the *headsail*.

Steerage way _____

Enough movement through the water to allow a boat to be steered.

Stem _____

The extreme leading edge of the hull of a boat.

Stem the tide _____

To make *headway* against a *current*.

Step a mast _____

To set up the *mast* and attach the *standing rigging*. The mast step is a socket or track at the base of the mast into which the mast butt is placed.

Stern _____

The back of the boat, or the *afterpart*.

The stern is surrounded by a rigid framework called a stern rail.

Stock

A crosspiece running between an anchor's hooks to give it better bite. Basically, the stock holds the anchor in place so that one of its *flukes* will bury itself. Many modern anchors have trigger devices instead of stocks to dig or force them into the seabed.

Storm sails, storm canvas

Strong, small sails for stormy weather, carried by the larger oceangoing sailboats. A storm *jib* is a small jib used for better control in bad weather, and the storm *trysail* replaces the *mainsail* during a threatening storm.

Detail of a storm sail, used in heavy weather.

Strategy

A general plan for a race, based on the wind, location, and *current*. See also *tactics*.

Stratus

See *clouds*.

Strike

To lower, as in striking a sail.

Surfing

To increase a boat's speed by riding waves, as a surfboard does.

Surge

A rhythmic motion along the *fore-and-aft* line caused by the motion of the waves.

Swamp

To fill up with water.

On a run in heavy weather the waves coming from behind will often pick up the boat and it will begin to surf.

Top: **The *Stars and Stripes*, an American 12-meter, racing in heavy swells.**

Above: **Tabernacle.**

Opposite page: **Close-hauled on port tack.**

Sweat

To haul up under tension.

Swell

Heavy rolling seas, caused by strong wind blowing at a distance; often a warning sign of a storm.

Tabernacle

A *deck* housing for the butt of a *mast*, often hinged to permit lowering the mast when passing under a bridge.

Tack

There are three different uses of the word tack. First, a tack is the lower forward corner of a sail. Second, a sailboat is always on the *port* or *starboard* tack, depending on which side of the boat the sails are on (the tack being the opposite side.) And third, a boat in the process of changing tacks by turning the *bow* of the boat into the wind is said to be tacking, or *coming about*.

© Dwight Ellefsen/Envision

Opposite page: Tackle.

**The crew has taken
in the mainsail, neatly
bundling and covering it.**

Tackle_____

A *purchase* system of
blocks and *lines* used
to gain a mechanical
advantage.

Tactics_____

The maneuvers used to
implement racing *strategy*
in light of the competition.
Also, the maneuvers with
which to prevent other
competitors from
implementing their strategy.

Tail_____

Generally, to haul on a line.
To tail is to pull hard on the
end of the *sheet* while
another crew member is
winching it in.

Take in_____

To lower or stow a *sail*.

Take up_____

To shorten or tighten
rigging.

Tall ships_____

A general term describing
the ships that traveled the
oceans by exploiting the
steady trade winds. The

nineteenth century brought
a great increase in world
trade; consequently there
was an increase in the size
of vessels built. Some of the
huge, square-rigged cargo
ships carried six or seven
masts.

*   *   *

These ocean-going square-
riggers, with their main
driving sails that lay square
to the mast, were especially
suited to sailing downwind.
In coastal waters where
winds are more variable,
square sails were combined
with a fore-and-aft rig
which, by setting sails
lengthwise along the vessel,
made it possible to sail a
square-rigged ship to
windward. Brigs,
brigantines, barks,
barkentines, and schooners
were among the faster,
more efficient vessels that
plied the coastlines.

*   *   *

The 1880s also saw the
introduction of the clipper
ship, although this was
more a new development in

hull shape than in rigging. Traders could choose between a vessel designed to carry a large cargo at a slow speed or a smaller cargo at a relatively faster speed. The clipper was designed in America, where speed was a priority, and in addition to its greater sail area, owed much of its speed to a further increase in length as compared to beam. Tea from China and wool from Australia were two special cargoes for which some famous clippers were built.

*　　*　　*

In one trade after another, the steamship began to usurp square-riggers. In the early twentieth century only one of the great trade routes was still open to sailing vessels—the route around Cape Horn for the South American nitrate trade. Steamships could not compete in those waters because of the scarcity of coaling stations and also because of the mechanical damage that affected propellers in the troughs of the enormous seas south of the Cape. The Panama Canal, opened in 1914, gave steamers the advantage there as well. Most of the large square-riggers still in service today are those used by several countries as training ships for naval cadets.

Tang

Metal fitting on a mast to which a *stay* is attached.

Telltales

Short pieces of yarn (commonly called woollies) attached to the *shrouds* that indicate wind direction. When attached to both sides of a sail, they allow the air flow over the sail to be checked, thus indicating how the sail should be trimmed.

Tender

A small boat kept on big yachts to be used at *anchorages* for expeditions to shore, to dock or to neighboring vessels.

Thermal

A rising column of warm air. See also *clouds*.

Thimble

A metal or plastic loop around which a *line* is wrapped to prevent chafing.

Three sheets to the wind

An old term referring to a sailor so drunk that even with three sheets to trim the sails, he would still be unable to manage his boat.

Thwart

A seat placed across a small boat.

The tall ships still in use today are often used as training vessels for naval cadets.

Tides

The vertical rise and fall of the ocean level caused by gravitational attraction—principally of the moon, and to a lesser extent, of the sun. In most regions this rise and fall happens twice each lunar day, which lasts about 24 hours and 50 minutes.

*   *   *

The Nautical Ocean Survey publishes four volumes of tide tables that cover the world. These tide tables are published annually and enable a navigator to predict the state of the tide for any place, date, and time.

Tide rips

See *rip*.

Tideway

Part of *channel* or fairway where the *current* runs the strongest.

Tight cover

In racing, a defensive position in front, or to *weather*, of a boat in which the lead boat aerodynamically slows the follower. Compare *loose cover*.

Tiller

A stick, usually made of metal or wood, attached to the *rudder* for steering. Steering wheels are generally used on large boats.

Tool kit

Fishing tackle boxes that are made out of heavy-duty plastic make great tool kits. A well-stocked marine tool kit should include:
- wire cutters
- tape measure
- vise grips
- adjustable wrench
- crescent wrenches
- variety of screwdrivers
- assortment of screws, nuts, bolts
- assortment of shackles
- hammer
- Nicopress swaging tool
- rivet gun
- putty knives
- sanding blocks
- sand paper
- sponges
- Exacto knife
- Knife with a marlinespike attachment

Topping lift

A line that holds up a boom when its sail is being set.

Topside

On deck.

Topsides

The sides of a boat between the *waterline* and the *deck*.

Tow

To pull behind a boat. A towline should be tied around the *mast* of the boat being towed. The *helmsman* should avoid letting the towline chafe against the *forestay*.

© Allan Weitz

Topside.

© Jim Tuten/FPG International

Left: Transom.

A good trapezing crew adjusts his or her position constantly to keep the boat sailing upright.

Trade wind

A dry wind blowing continuously in a belt about thirty degrees north and south of the equator. The hot air in this region rises into the atmosphere, and the heavier surrounding air blows in to fill the void. The trade winds in the northern hemisphere come from the northeast, and in the southern hemisphere from the southeast.

Trailers

Metal rigs pulled by cars or trucks that carry boats on land; used by those who keep their boats at home or sailors who travel with their boats.

Transom

The flat surface across the *stern*; the stern facing of the *hull*.

Trapeze

A *hiking* system that suspends the crew outside a racing dinghy by wires running from the *mast* to a hook on a trapeze harness. Using a handle on the trapeze wire and the *jib sheet* to balance, a skillful crew can move rapidly in and out of the boat according to wind shifts and *course* changes.

Traveler

A slide that runs on a track across the boat and is used to control the *mainsail leech* tension.

Trim

The angle of a sail to the wind direction. To trim a *sail* is to pull it in using the *sheet;* opposite of *ease.*

Trimaran

A boat with three hulls.

Trough

The valley between the crests of waves.

True wind

The actual direction the wind is blowing across the water. The wind felt under sail is the *apparent wind.* The apparent wind is forward of the true wind.

Trysail

A small triangular sail used to replace the *mainsail* in heavy weather; a *storm sail.*

Turnbuckle

A fitting used to maintain the proper tension on *shrouds* and *stays.*

Turn turtle

To *capsize* by turning completely over so that the *mast* points down to the bottom. See also *capsize.*

Under the lee

Protected from the wind by a cape, another boat, a wooded *point,* or any wind-blocking object.

Upwind

Toward the direction from which the breeze is blowing.

Vane

A wind indicator on the *masthead;* Also called a *masthead fly.*

Vang

See *boom vang.*

Variation

The difference between true north and magnetic north, which is expressed in degrees.

Veering

A clockwise change in wind direction—south to south-west, for example. Compare *backing.*

Opposite page: **Traveler.**

Veer and haul

Slackening and then pulling a rope in a rhythmic motion.

Voyage

A sea journey that generally includes outward and return *passage*.

Wake

Disturbed water left behind a moving boat.

Warp

To maneuver a boat into a desired position by using *lines* extended to dock or shore.

Watch

A working shift aboard a vessel.

Waterline

The straight-line distance from the point where the *bow* emerges from the water to the point where the *stern* emerges from the water.

Way

Movement through the water by motor power or wind power.

The frothy path left behind a moving boat is called the wake.

Weather

The area to *windward*, or *upwind*.

Weather helm

The tendency of a boat to head into the wind if the helm is dropped.

Weather lore

Here are some of the signs and portents handed down by sailors over time as weather indicators:

* * *

When seagulls fly out in the morning far to seaward, the weather should be fair. When those birds stay close to the shore, expect strong winds and possible storms.

* * *

Look for rapid wind changes by observing smoke from leaf fires, factories, or trailing from ships. Smoke streaming downwind from its source indicates dropping pressure and likely rain. Smoke rising upward in a column indicates good weather.

* * *

Rhymes have long served as devices for predicting the weather:

"Rainbow at night is the sailor's delight / Rainbow at morning, sailors take warning." (This rhyme also applies to "Red sky at night..."

"Mackerel skies and mares' tails make tall ships carry small sails."

Above: **Watching the behavior of sea gulls and other pelagic birds aids in understanding the weather.**

Opposite page: **Winch.**

"Seagull, seagull, sit on the sand / It's never good when you're on land."

"When the wind shifts against the sun / Trust it not for back it will run. / When the wind follows the sun / Fine weather will never be done."

"Rain long foretold, long last / Short notice, soon past."

Weather shore_____
Land or shore toward which the wind blows.

Weigh anchor_____
To raise the anchor from the seabed.

Whipping_____
Twine wrapped tightly around the end of a line to prevent fraying or unraveling.

Whisker pole_____
A *spar* used to hold out the *jib* when *goosewinged.*

Winch_____
A reellike fitting mounted on the deck of a boat that provides extra *purchase* for *trimming sheets* and raising *halyards.*

Windage

The amount of sail area exposed to the wind. Also, the boat's surface that is exposed to the wind.

Wind indicator

See *masthead fly*.

Windjammer

A colloquial term for a *square-rigger,* originally used contemptuously by sailors on steamships.

Windlass

A machine for hoisting or hauling cable, chain, or heavy *line*.

Wind shadow

The air directly to *leeward* of a sail.

© C. Protopapas

Above: **Square-rigged sailing vessels are often called windjammers.**

Right: **A wind indicator will measure the change in the direction of the apparent wind.**

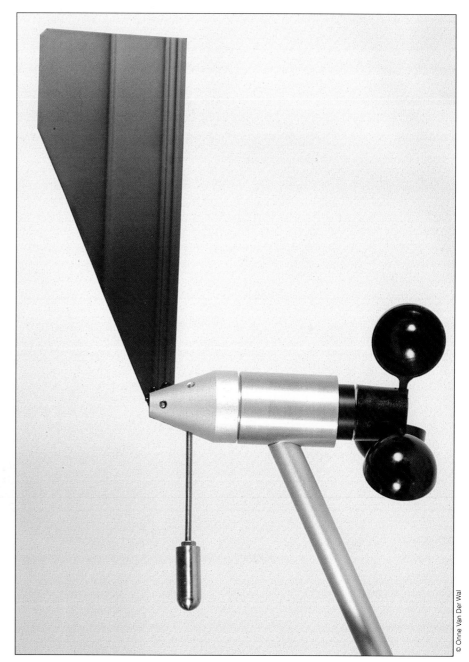

© Onne Van Der Wal

Windsurfing

An increasingly popular sport (which became an Olympic event in 1984) invented by California surfers who tired of having to paddle out to the big waves. Some say that windsurfing is one of a handful of truly original ideas to appear in sailing over the past years.

Windward

The direction from which the wind is blowing; opposite of *leeward*.

Wing and wing

See *goosewing*.

Woolies

See *telltales*.

© Christopher Bain

Windsurfing has become a popular pastime in recent years.

Wreck

The hull of a ship rendered completely useless. Curiously, a ship driven on the rocks or shore is technically not deemed a wreck if a crew member or even a pet survives the calamity.

Below: Wreck.

Y

Yacht

General term for a pleasure boat that fits both sail- and power-driven boats.

© Allan Weitz

A cruising yawl.

Z

Yard

The *spar* from which a
square *sail* is suspended.
The tapering end of a yard
is known as the yardarm.

Yaw

To turn accidentally from
the intended course, often
as a result of heavy seas.

Yawl

A double-masted sailboat in
which the *mizzenmast* is
aft of the point where the
rudderpost intersects the
waterline. See *Sailboat rig*.

Zephyr

The west wind; any gentle
warm breeze.

Zigzagging

Sailing continuously on
alternate *tacks* of approximately equal distance.

Appendices

Beaufort Wind Scale

Beaufort Scale	Description and Wind Speed (in knots)	Effects seen at sea	Effects seen on land
0	calm less than 1	sea like a mirror	smoke rises vertically
1	light air 1–3	small ripples	smoke drifts, weather vanes do not move
2	light breeze 4-6	small wavelets	leaves rustle, vanes move, breeze felt on face
3	gentle breeze 7–10	large wavelets, crests begin to break, occasional whitecaps	leaves in constant motion, light flags extended
4	moderate breeze 11–16	small waves (0.5–1.25 meters high), whitecaps numerous	small branches move, dust and loose paper may be raised
5	fresh breeze 17–21	moderate waves (1.5–2.5 meters high), many whitecaps, some spray	small trees sway, tops of all trees in motion
6	strong breeze 22–27	larger waves (2.5–4 meters), whitecaps everywhere, more spray	larger tree branches in motion, whistling heard through wires
7	near gale 28–33	waves 4–6 meters, white foam from breaking waves begins to be blown	whole trees in motion

Beaufort Scale	Description and Wind Speed (in knots)	Effects seen at sea	Effects seen on land
8	gale 34–40	moderately high waves (4–6 meters) of greater length, edges of crests begin to break into spin-drift, foam is blown in well-defined streaks	twigs broken off trees, impeded progress on foot
9	strong gale 41–47	high waves (6 meters), sea starts to roll, spray may reduce visibility	fences blown down, shingles blown from roofs
10	storm 48–55	very high waves (6–9 meters) with overhanging crests heavily rolling seas, reduced visibility	rarely experienced on land; trees broken or uprooted, considerable structural damage
11	violent storm 56-63	exceptionally high waves (9–14 meters) sea covered with white foam patches	
12	hurricane 64 upwards	air filled with foam, waves over 14 meters, sea completely white with driving spray, visibility greatly reduced	

APPENDIX II

Common Abbreviations

AC: Alternating current.

ADF: Automatic direction finder.
A sophisticated type of radio direction finder.

BIA: Boating Industries Association.
A trade organization that helps set safety standards.

C: Course.
Used in marking charts. Also Celsius, or Centigrade, usually written as °C.

CB: Compass bearing.
Also, Citizen's Band, *a shortwave radio frequency band.*

CMG: Course made good.

CNG: Compressed natural gas.
Used for heating.

COLREGS: *Coast Guard term for* International Regulations for the Prevention of Collisions at Sea.

CQR: "Secure."
A patented brand of anchor.

D: Direction, *or* distance.
Used in marking charts.

DC: Direct current.

DF: Direction finder.

DR: Dead reckoning.

EP: Estimated position.

EPIRB: Emergency position indicating radio beacon.

ETA: Estimated time of arrival.

ETD: Estimated time of departure.

F: Fix.
Also, Fahrenheit, *usually written as °F.*

GMT: Greenwich Mean Time.

HIN: Hull identification number.

hp: Horsepower.

ICW: Intracoastal waterway.

km: Kilometer *(1,000 meters). Equal to approximately ⅝ of a mile.*

kn: Knot.
One nautical mile per hour.

lat.: Latitude.

LLW: Lower low water.

LOA: Length overall.

long.: Longitude.

LOP: Line of position.

LW: Low water.
Found on charts.

LWL: Load waterline, *or* length on the waterline.

MHW: Mean high water.

NW: Notice to Mariners.

PFD: Personal flotation device.
A life jacket or buoyant cushion.

RDF: Radio direction finder.

rpm: Revolutions per minute.

SAR: "Search and rescue."

SOS: Morse code distress signal.

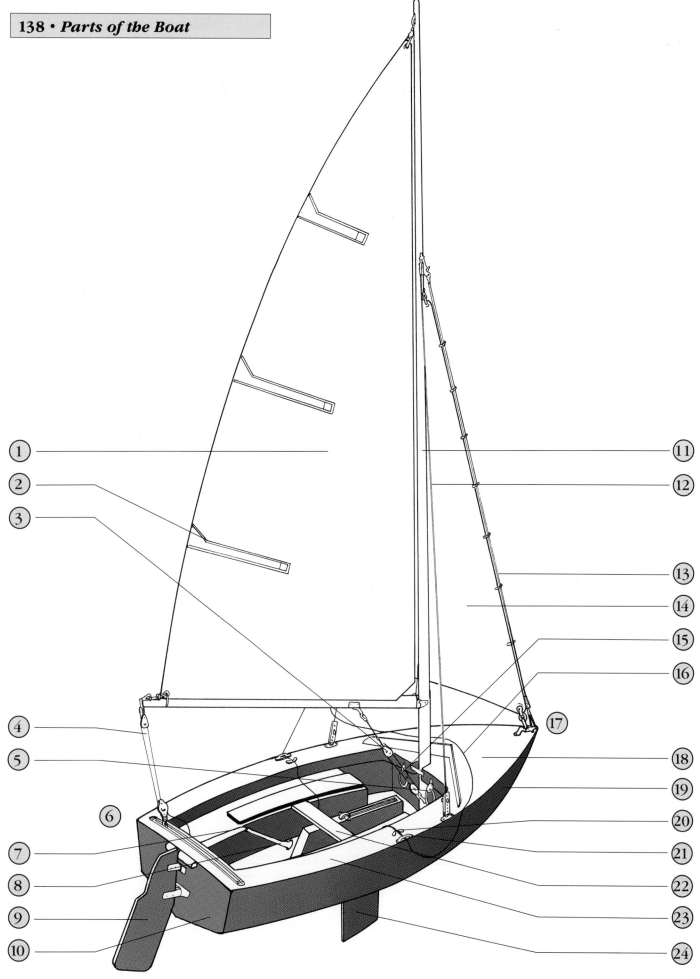

APPENDIX III

Parts of the Boat

①	Mainsail	⑬	Headstay
②	Batten pocket	⑭	Jib
③	Boom vang	⑮	Jib halyard
④	Mainsheet	⑯	Jib sheets
⑤	Mainsail halyard	⑰	Bow
⑥	Stern	⑱	Foredeck
⑦	Tiller	⑲	Hull
⑧	Tiller extension	⑳	Cleats
⑨	Rudder	㉑	Fairlead
⑩	Transom	㉒	Thwart
⑪	Mast	㉓	Side-deck
⑫	Shroud	㉔	Centerboard

Further Reading

Boatbuilding and Design

Brewer, Ted. **Ted Brewer Explains Sailboat Design.** Camden, Maine: International Marine, 1985.

Greene, Danny. **Cruising Sailboat Kinetics: The Art, Science, and Magic of Cruising Boat Design.** Blue Ridge Summit, Pennsylvania: TAB Books, 1985.

Mellor, John, **Sailing Cruiser Manual.** Dobbs Ferry, New York: Sheridan House, 1989.

Roberts, John. **Fiberglass Boats: Construction, Repair, Maintenance.** New York: W.W. Norton, 1984.

Taube, Allen: **The Boatbuilder's Companion.** Camden, Maine: International Marine, 1985.

Wood, Charles E. **Building Your Dream Boat.** Centreville, Maryland: Cornell Maritime Press, 1981.

Cruising

Betterley, Joan. **Good Food Afloat.** Camden, Maine: International Marine, 1986.

Cornell, Gwenda. **Cruising with Children.** Adlard Coles; distr. Sheridan House, Dobbs Ferry, New York, 1986.

Cornell, Jimmy. **World Cruising Routes.** Camden, Maine: International Marine, 1987.

Hiscock, Eric. **Cruising Under Sail.** 3rd ed. Camden, Maine: International Marine, 1986.

Lucas, Alan. **Cruising in Tropical Waters and Coral.** Camden, Maine: International Marine, 1987.

Marshall, Roger. **Cruising Techniques Illustrated.** New York: W.W. Norton, 1989.

Parton, Nicole. **Nicole Parton's Galley Gourmet: Great Meals from Small Spaces.** Seattle, Washington: Pacific Search Press, 1987.

Skoog, Jim. **Cruising in Comfort.** Camden, Maine: International Marine, 1986.

First Aid

Beilan, Dr. Michael H. **Your Offshore Doctor: A Manual of Medical Self-Sufficiency at Sea.** New York: Putnam Publishing Group, 1986.

Kessler: Dr. William. **Medical Emergencies at Sea; A Manual for the Cruising Yachtsman.** New York: William Morrow, 1986.

Knots

Bigon, Mario, and Regazzoni, Guido. **The Morrow Guide to Knots.** New York: William Morrow, 1982.

Budworth, Geoffrey. **The Knot Book.** New York: Sterling, 1985.

Nautical History

Aymor, Brandt, ed. **Men at Sea: The Best Sea Stories of All Time, from Homer to William F. Buckley, Jr.** New York: Crown Publishers, 1988.

Harland, John. **Seamanship in the Age of Sail: An Account of the Sea Handling of the Man-of-War, 1600–1860.** Annapolis, Maryland: Naval Institute Press, 1984.

Hendrickson, Robert. **The Ocean Almanac.** New York: Doubleday, 1988.

Slocum, Joshua. **Sailing Alone Around the World.** Orig. pub. 1900. New York: Dover, 1956.

Throckmorton, Peter. **The Sea Remembers.** New York: Grove Press, 1987.

Navigation

Arnold, David. **Tides and Currents.** Camden, Maine: International Marine, 1986.

Bergin, Edward J. **A Star to Steer Her By: A Self-Teaching Guide to Offshore Navigation.** Centreville, Maryland: Cornell Maritime Press, 1983.

Blewitt, Mary. **Celestial Navigation for Yachtsmen.** New York: Philosophical Library, 1955.

Bowditch, Nathaniel. **American Practical Navigator.** 2 vol. Orig. pub. in 1802. Washington, DC: Defense Mapping Agency Hydrographic/Topographic Center, 1984.

Eldridge Tide and Pilot Book 1989. Boston, Massachusetts: Robert Eldridge White, Publisher, 1988.

Fraser, Bruce. **The Weekend Navigator.** Clinton Corners, New York: John de Graff, 1981.

Maloney, Elbert S. **Dutton's Navigation and Piloting.** 14th ed. Annapolis, Maryland: Naval Institute Press, 1985.

Markell, Jeff. **Coastal Navigation for the Small Boat Sailor.** Blue Ridge Summit, Pennsylvania: TAB Books, 1984.

Melton, Luke. **The Complete Loran-C Handbook.** Camden Maine: International Marine, 1986.

Shufeldt, H.H., and Dunlap, G. B. **Piloting and Dead Reckoning.** 2nd ed. Annapolis, Maryland: Naval Institute Press, 1981.

U.S. Government Printing Office. **Nautical Almanac for the Year 1989.** Washington, DC: Government Printing Office, 1989.

Racing

Colgate, Steve. **Manual of Racing Techniques.** City Island, New York: Offshore Sailing School, 1975.

Melges, Buddy, and Mason, Charles. **Sailing Smart: Winning Techniques, Tactics, and Strategies.** New York: Holt, Rinehart and Winston, 1983.

Perry, Dave. **Understanding the Yacht Racing Rules Through 1992.** New York: Putnam Publishing Group, 1989.

_____ . **Winning in One-Designs.** New York: Dodd, Mead, 1984.

Twiname, Eric. **Sail, Race, and Win.** Charlestown, Massachusetts: Sail Publications, 1982.

_____ . **Start to Win.** 2nd ed. Adlard Coles; distr. Sheridan House, Dobbs Ferry, New York, 1983.

Walker, Stuart H. **A Manual of Sail Trim.** New York: W. W. Norton, 1984.

_____ . **Winning: The Psychology of Competition.** New York: W. W. Norton, 1986.

Seamanship and Sailing Theory

Colgate, Steve. **Manual of Basic Sailing Theory.** City Island, New York: Offshore Sailing School, 1973.

Henderson, Richard. **Sailing at Night.** Camden, Maine: International Marine, 1987.

_____ . **Understanding Rigs and Rigging.** Camden, Maine: International Marine, 1987.

Hinz, Earl. **The Complete Book of Anchoring and Mooring.** Centreville, Maryland: Cornell Maritime Press, 1986.

Johnson, Gary. **Sailing Fundamentals.** New York: Simon and Schuster, 1987.

Langley-Price, Pat, and Ourvy, Philip. **Competent Crew: An Introduction to the Practice and Theory of Sailing.** London: Adlard Coles, 1985.

Maloney, Elbert S. **Chapman Piloting, Seamanship and Small Boat Handling.** 58th ed. New York: Hearst Corporation, 1987.

Rousmaniere, John. **Annapolis Book of Seamanship.** New York: Simon and Schuster, 1983.

Weather

Coles, K. Adlard. **Heavy Weather Sailing.** 3rd rev. ed. New York: John de Graff, 1981.

Dunlop, Storm, and Wilson, Francis. **Weather and Forecasting.** New York: MacMillan, 1982.

Watts, Alan. **Instant Wind Forecasting.** Adlard Coles; distr. Sheridan House, Dobbs Ferry, New York, 1988.

_____ . **Reading the Weather: Modern Techniques for Yachtsmen.** New York: Dodd, Mead, 1987.